Arnulfo L. Oliveira Memorial Library

Charles Goodnight

THE OKLAHOMA WESTERN BIOGRAPHIES
RICHARD W. ETULAIN, GENERAL EDITOR

Charles Goodnight

Father of the Texas Panhandle

William T. Hagan

UNIVERSITY OF OKLAHOMA PRESS : NORMAN

Also by William T. Hagan

The Sac and Fox Indians (Norman, 1958 and 1980)
American Indians (Chicago, 1961; rev. eds. 1979 and 1993)
Indian Police and Judges (New Haven, 1966; Lincoln, 1980)
United States–Comanche Relations (New Haven, 1976; Norman, 1990)
The Indian Rights Association (Tucson, 1985)
Quanah Parker, Comanche Chief (Norman, 1993)
Theodore Roosevelt and Six Friends of the Indian (Norman, 1997)
Taking Indian Lands (Norman, 2003)

Library of Congress Cataloging-in-Publication Data
Hagan, William Thomas.
Charles Goodnight : father of the Texas Panhandle / William T. Hagan.
p. cm. — (The Oklahoma western biographies)
Includes bibliographical references and index.
ISBN 978-0-8061-3827-5 (hardcover : alk. paper)
ISBN 978-0-8061-3882-4 (pbk. : alk. paper)
1. Goodnight, Charles, 1836–1929. 2. Ranchers—Texas—Biography.
3. Ranch life—Texas—History. 4. J.A. Ranch (Tex.)—History.
5. Rangelands—Texas—History. 6. Cattle trade—Texas—History.
7. Pioneers—Texas—Texas Panhandle—Biography. 8. Frontier and pioneer
life—Texas—Texas Panhandle. 9. Texas Panhandle (Tex.)—History. I. Title.
F391.G66H34 2007
976.4'04092—dc22
[B]   2007004248

Charles Goodnight: Father of the Texas Panhandle is Volume 21 in The
Oklahoma Western Biographies.

1   2   3   4   5   6   7   8   9   10

To the ever-helpful John Lovett

Contents

Illustrations

Photographs

Maps

Series Editor's Foreword

STORIES of heroes and heroines have intrigued many generations of listeners and readers. Americans, like people everywhere, have been captivated by the lives of military, political, and religious figures and of intrepid explorers, pioneers, and rebels. The Oklahoma Western Biographies endeavor to build on this fascination with biography and to link it with two other abiding interests of Americans: the frontier and the American West. Although volumes in the series carry no notes, they are prepared by leading scholars, are soundly researched, and include a list of sources used. Each volume is a lively synthesis based on thorough examination of pertinent primary and secondary sources.

Above all, The Oklahoma Western Biographies aim at two goals: to provide readable life stories of significant Westerners and to show how their lives illuminate a notable topic, an influential movement, or a series of important events in the history and culture of the American West.

William T. Hagan's appealing new biography of Charles Goodnight (1836–1929) provides a colorful account of one of the American West's preeminent ranchers. Who more than Goodnight epitomizes the courageous, indefatigable, physical presence of the cowboy, drover, and cattleman of Texas? Hagan clearly illustrates the gargantuan strengths and limitations of this gruff, largely self-educated, and driven cattle baron.

Some readers will particularly enjoy the author's humorous treatment of Goodnight's fantastic methods of cattle breeding. Others will be fascinated with the cattleman's unorthodox bovine surgeries. No one should miss, either, the startling contraditions of this huge, vulgar, and cigar-chewing cattle king who regularly, and easily, fired men for gambling and drinking.

Hagan also perceptively points out the complicated webs of connections that enmeshed Goodnight. We learn of his entangling alliances with English and eastern financiers, his links with other Texas Panhandle cattlemen, and his ties to men and women attempting to organize and "civilize" West Texas. Some of these complicated alignments arose from Goodnight's stubborn desire to keep decision-making close at hand rather than with the "suits, shirts, and ties" of snooty, ambitious men in faraway Austin.

Glimpses of Goodnight's ranch and home life likewise enliven Hagan's biography. Devoted to his wife, Mary, to whom he was married more than fifty years, Goodnight saluted her fortitude and loyalty by remarking once, "What would I do without her?" Yet not long after her death, the ninety-one-year-old Goodnight took as a new bride Corrine Goodnight, a distant relative. According to this second wife, Goodnight was "a wonderful man. . . . Kindness and goodness, 'Personified.'"

This new, readable biography of Charles Goodnight fulfills the two major goals of the Oklahoma Western Biographies series. It is a clear, appealing story of a notable Western figure, and it reveals how Goodnight's life and career illuminate larger themes in the history of the American West.

RICHARD W. ETULAIN

University of New Mexico

Preface

MY interest in Charles Goodnight grew out of my curiosity about the unusual environment of the Texas Panhandle. I was first attracted to the area in the 1960s when I attended a theatrical production there that featured Charles Goodnight as a character in a supporting role. This was my first exposure to the Palo Duro Canyon and the Staked Plains. Some thirty years later, I was in the audience for another production of the same show. By that time I was retired and was able to indulge my curiosity about the canyon and the plains above it, the largest flat area in the Western Hemisphere.

It is impossible to learn more about the area without becoming aware of Charles Goodnight's pivotal role in the development of the Panhandle. As a result, somewhere along the way I decided to attempt a study of the early occupation of the area by cattlemen, with an emphasis on the role of Goodnight. That J. Evetts Haley's splendid biography of him was still in print would normally have given me pause. But, as a retiree I now enjoy the luxury of pursuing whatever interests me, without regard to the need to further my professional career. And Haley had written relatively little on Goodnight's last thirty years.

Over the last several years I have satisfied my curiosity about the nature of ranching in the settlement of the Texas Panhandle, and have become acquainted with the people, and particularly Goodnight, who played a pivotal role in that era. As one who himself is coping with the aging process, I have been interested in how Goodnight dealt with the situation. He had always had more energy than the average man and an intense interest in all aspects of his environment.

I am greatly indebted to those who have preceded me in the field, and they are listed in the Sources section at the end of this volume. In the course of my own research, a number of people have been very helpful. They include John Lovett, of the Western History Collections of the University of Oklahoma; Betty L. Bustos, of the Panhandle Plains Museum; Jim Bradshaw, of the Haley Library and History Center; David W. Parrish, of Geneseo, New York; Tara Wenger, of the Harry Ransom Humanities Center of the University of Texas at Austin; and the staff of the Center of American History, also of the University of Texas at Austin. The staff at the University of Oklahoma's Bizzell Library was ever-courteous and helpful, and Doni J. Fox, a Bizzell Library staff member, provided valuable assistance on the maps. My daughter, Sarah Esser, provided tutelage on computer operation at a critical time. And my wife, Charlotte (April) Hagan, was the source, as always, of the ambience enabling me to do my work.

Charles Goodnight

CHAPTER I

Becoming a Man

WHEN he died in 1929 at the age of ninety-three, Goodnight had outlived almost all of his fellow participants in the opening of the Texas Panhandle. He had become a living legend, an icon at whose feet one could learn of an era now glamorized in a surge of nostalgia for the pioneer days.

Certainly no one would have predicted celebrity for the nine-year-old youngster who in 1845 had ridden bareback eight hundred miles from Illinois with his family to what would be the first of several hardscrabble farms in Texas. Goodnight's was the common experience for a youth struggling to survive on the frontier. As he recalled in his later years: "I rarely think of my childhood days. . . . I had no special ambition; not a single plan that I can recall; just lived along like other boys; devilish poor; had to work all the time just for a living." Thus it is no surprise that Goodnight's formal education was limited to two terms in a rural Illinois school, and he was never able to read and write with any facility. His early experience with poverty and drudgery, however, taught him the value of a dollar and spurred him to seize any opportunity to get ahead.

As a young teenager Goodnight moved on from the usual chores on the family farm to work as a hired hand for other farmers to supplement the family income. His first real job required him to walk to and from a farm two miles away, and the pay was only four dollars a month. But he proved his worth, and as he grew he was given more responsibilities, and his wages rose accordingly. Before he branched out on his own, Goodnight was earning twenty-five dollars a month.

His first real education as a rider came in the form of an

unbroken mustang colt. As an old man he remembered that he had not had a saddle, and the mustang threw him "hundreds of times," but never ran away. "I became much attached to this wild mustang." Not until the boy was a couple of years older did he acquire a saddle of his own, a reward for helping a drover recover his runaway cattle from a stretch of timber. By the age of fifteen, his riding skills and then-small frame earned him brief employment as a jockey.

In the next few years Goodnight graduated to working with cattle and began freighting, in which he engaged off and on until 1865. Driving ox-drawn wagons as a bull whacker could be a frustrating experience that undoubtedly helped him develop the highly profane vocabulary for which he was noted throughout his adult life.

In the mid-1850s the family located in the Cross Timbers in north-central Texas. The region offered sufficient good, free range to become the birthplace of some of the most prominent ranching operations in the state. Here, families like the Waggoners, Burnettes, and Ikards would emerge as local cattle kings. In contrast to Goodnight, all these ranchers came from families with sufficient financial resources to help launch them in the business.

Goodnight's entry into ranching came by chance. When he was twenty, he and a step-brother, John Wesley Sheek, determined that their future lay in California. The summer of 1856 the two young men actually headed west, only to be held up not far from home by a flooded stream. By the time it was fordable they had met a relative of Sheek's, Claiborn Varner, who talked them into becoming co-owners with him of a herd of about four hundred longhorns. Goodnight and Sheek contracted for five years, later extended to ten, to take responsibility for the herd in return for half the annual calf crop. They drove the herd to the Black Springs area on Keechi Creek in Palo Pinto County, on what was then Texas's northwest frontier. The county would become the home of several prominent ranching families such as the Slaughters and the Hittsons.

The first year of Goodnight and Sheek's contract with Varner, the calf crop was disappointingly small, but at the end of their second contract, they had accumulated, with some purchases on the side, about 6,000 head. They then bought out Varner's share in the herd. The census of 1860 listed them with property, presumably cattle, worth $1,250 each.

Three years after the young men located in Palo Pinto County, the parents decided to join them and reunite the family on Keechi Creek. With Charlie playing the lead role, they erected a large log cabin, actually two cabins joined by a breezeway. It became, in addition to being a residence, a tavern for travelers on the road from Weatherford, Texas, to New Mexico.

At that time most of north-central Texas was free range, open to occupancy by the first cattleman brave enough to stake out his claim. Palo Pinto County continued to attract a number of stockmen, including Oliver Loving, already a major figure in the cattle business. The 1860 census recorded his affluence. He was listed as forty-eight years of age and a trader with property worth $2,000 and a total estate of $25,440.

Palo Pinto County, however, was less than fifty miles from two American Indian reservations. The closest was home to several nonthreatening farming and hunting tribes, among them the Wichitas and Caddos. But the other reservation was occupied by Penateka Comanches, buffalo Indians. Other Comanches were still roaming the South Plains, periodically raiding Texas frontier settlements, killing settlers, carrying off women and children, and driving off cattle and horses. Rarely was there accurate identification of the raiders, but outraged settlers accused the reservation Comanches of either participating in the assaults or, at a minimum, providing the raiders a supply base.

Charles Goodnight had his first experience with American Indians in the late 1850s. He quickly established a reputation for possessing the qualities of a scout: excellent vision and woods and plains craft that enabled him to track raiding parties. He attributed his abilities to a lifetime outdoors, although that was a background common to most young Texans. Goodnight was clearly better endowed and had a deeper interest in nature in all of its manifestations.

The response of the federal government to the increasing Indian threat to settlement along the Texas frontier had been the construction of a chain of forts, beginning in 1851. These were beyond the Cross Timbers and on the eastern edge of the Rolling Plains, which extended west to the ramparts of the Staked Plains. The first wave of settlers in Palo Pinto County took some comfort from the presence of Fort Belknap, some forty miles northwest of Black Springs. Unfortunately, the garrisons of the forts were usually too small, or made up of infantry and artillerymen — no threat to horse Indians. Historian David Paul Smith has uncovered a relevant statement by journalist Frederick Law Olmstead: "Keeping a bulldog to chase mosquitoes would be of no greater nonsense than stationing six-pounders, bayonets, and dragoons for the pursuit of these red wolves."

In 1858 the raids on the Texas frontier had intensified, and the settlers tended to place much of the blame on the occupants of the two reservations on the Upper Brazos, particularly the Comanches. A principal agitator for a military solution was John R. Baylor, himself a former agent for the Texas Comanches. In 1859 he raised a force of settlers and marched on the Comanche reservation. Among his recruits was Charles Goodnight. Decades later he remembered that when they had reached the reservation they found it protected by federal troops, and withdrew. But it had become apparent in Washington that the only solution palatable to its Texas citizens was the removal to Indian Territory, north of Red River, of the populations of the two Texas reservations. That was accomplished in the fall of 1859, but it did not end the raids on the Texas frontier.

The response of the state authorities in Austin consisted mostly of authorizations of units to be raised among the frontier population. One of the volunteers was again Goodnight, who participated in some of the expeditions against the Indians. The best-known of these resulted in the Pease River Battle in December 1860. It came after continued Indian raids had forced Governor Sam Houston to authorize L. S. "Sul" Ross to raise a company of rangers.

Captain Ross's rangers were reinforced by a small detachment of regulars, plus additional volunteers from the local population. They rendezvoused at Fort Belknap, no longer garrisoned by regular troops. Here, Ross mustered into service a few more volunteers, including Charles Goodnight. Because of his familiarity with the area, Goodnight was asked to serve as scout and guide. This was his first official service in that capacity.

Years later, he summarized for J. Frank Dobie, a University of Texas authority on Southwest folklore and history, the qualities of a good scout. First of all, he must be able to approximate the direction, and distance to, the nearest water source. Goodnight's estimates were based on a range of factors, including the nature of local plant life and the actions of animals and birds. The presence of mustangs, for example, would indicate water within three miles, as they seldom ranged farther than that from water.

Following a horse's trail, Goodnight could determine the age of the track by checking the condition of grass trampled by the horse's hooves and any disturbance of insect activity. The nature of the hoofprints also would inform him as to whether or not the horse had a rider, or was being led. Finally, the color of the mount might be determined by hair left on the ground when the horse rolled after being unsaddled, as horses customarily did.

The good scout also had to be able to identify animal sounds and distinguish between the real turkey call and what could be the effort of an Indian to fake one. The scout must have the knack for approximating the direction from which the sound was coming and stay on that tack, regardless of terrain changes. Goodnight believed that few men had that capacity or "instinct." He did, and despite never possessing a compass, was never completely lost.

When they pulled out of Fort Belknap, Goodnight led the detachment in a northwest direction, and quickly intercepted a trail that he had located on an earlier reconnaissance with another detachment. Only two days out, they reached an Indian encampment on the Pease River, in present-day Foard County.

The surprised Indians were in the act of breaking camp, and the sudden attack sent them fleeing in disorder. The troops quickly overtook and killed them, except for a woman and her infant daughter, whom they took captive.

The mother was Cynthia Ann Parker, whom Comanches had abducted as a nine-year-old, when they attacked Fort Parker in East Texas in 1836. Subsequently she had become the wife of an Indian man and the mother of three children, the oldest being Quanah, who would become the most-celebrated Comanche chief of all time. As he rose to prominence, members of the Sul Ross command would boast of having been present at his mother's recapture, and dispute with Goodnight his claim to have been the first to identify Cynthia Ann as a white woman.

Within a year of the Pease River skirmish, the Civil War would be underway, and Indian attacks on the Texas frontier would intensify. Federal authorities in Indian Territory no longer had an incentive to restrain the raiders, and indeed, encouraged attacks on the rebels. Goodnight would be involved in trying to protect the Texas frontier, as he missed service in the Confederate Army because he had been on crutches from a leg injury when the initial recruitment occurred. Subsequently, able-bodied young men were permitted the alternative of enlisting for frontier duty. Goodnight served in that capacity off and on throughout the war. When he was on active duty, he scouted for ranger units as far west as the eastern escarpment of the Llano Estacado (Staked Plains) in the Texas Panhandle.

Goodnight's service was so irregular as to permit him to keep an eye on the Goodnight-Sheek herd as it continued to multiply. Indeed, in the early sixties it had reached the size that their old pasture near Black Springs could no longer support the entire herd, and he drove 3,000 head fifty miles northwest to Throckmorton County, where he found good grazing for them.

There was a downside to this. It complicated his courtship of the schoolteacher at Black Springs, Mary Ann Dyer. A pretty, black-haired girl in her late twenties, she was that rarity on the frontier, an attractive, single female of marriageable age. Indeed, most girls married in their teens in a frontier society that always had a preponderance of young males. But Mary, as Goodnight always referred to her, had as her first responsibility, after the death of both parents, the care of three younger brothers. Goodnight, however, was persistent. Even her relocation to Weatherford, a settlement about twenty-five miles from Black Springs, did not deter his courtship. The local people were intrigued by the odd couple — the uneducated and uncouth cattleman and the petite and very feminine school teacher, Miss Dyer.

The end of the war, in 1865, and the resumption of more settled conditions did not alter the pace of their relationship. But, hopefully, peace would present opportunities for Goodnight and Sheek to finally cash in on their cattle holdings. Goodnight was prepared for any opportunity. He was now an experienced cattleman, and was recognized as having the skills, strength, and endurance to cope with the challenges that accompanied life on the frontier.

CHAPTER 2

Cattle Drover and Colorado Rancher

IN 1860 Texas was estimated to be the range for 3,786,433 cattle, but only one-sixth that many people. During the war, markets for those cattle were gradually cut off by the Union blockade of Texas ports, the fall of New Orleans into Union hands, and a stronger Union presence in Indian Territory. Meanwhile, the cattle continued to multiply, and most of the increase was unbranded and under no control. Charles Goodnight and Wes Sheek lost many of their cattle as they drifted away, or were driven off by local rustlers or Indians. One of their herdsmen had died at the hands of Indians in the summer of 1864. A few weeks later Goodnight got revenge by killing a warrior, one of a party driving off stolen horses. He was in hot pursuit of the fleeing Indian when the warrior's horse was killed by another ranger. But he hit the ground running, turning briefly to fire one arrow at Goodnight. That gave Goodnight time to put two revolver rounds in the Indian, and he was dead — "a good Indian" as Goodnight phrased it.

The raids that fall were especially intense. Goodnight estimated that the local cattlemen had lost ten thousand head. Such financial blows forced the Texans to consider other ranching sites. At the end of the Civil War they made a party to explore the ranching possibilities in Old Mexico. The party of six included Christopher C. "Lum" Slaughter, who had been with Goodnight in the ranger party that recaptured Cynthia Ann Parker. Only a few miles from the Rio Grande, the party was riding single file through a cedar break when one man's rifle was entangled in brush and fired, seriously wounding Slaughter. He would recover, but that terminated their expedition to Mexico.

In the spring of 1866 Goodnight, still looking for a means to capitalize on the surplus of cattle in north-central Texas, discussed the problem with a neighbor and a leading figure in Palo Pinto County, Oliver Loving, whom Goodnight liked and respected. The younger man was planning a drive of a thousand head that would reduce the chances of encountering Plains Indians by "taking roundance," by traveling southwest on the Old Butterfield Overland Mail route to a crossing of the Pecos River. Once beyond that, he proposed to head north to Fort Sumner. There the army was holding—and feeding—about eight thousand Navajos, and had advertised for beef on the hoof.

Loving was by far the more experienced cattleman, having driven herds north, including one that in 1860 pioneered a trail across Indian Territory and on to Colorado. Goodnight had accompanied that drive, but only as far as Red River. Now Loving decided to accept the lead of the younger man, and put together another thousand head to match Goodnight's. The combined herds included a mix of steers, cows, and young stock. They agreed on a rough division of responsibilities. Loving, at fifty-five the elder and more experienced in marketing cattle, would take the lead in financial matters while Goodnight, twenty years younger and a veteran scout, would concentrate on organizing and conducting the drive. It fell to him to assign duties to the sixteen hands recruited and oversee their performance.

Goodnight was a demanding boss, approaching every task himself with all the energy he could muster, and he expected the same dedicated work habits from those under his direction. Several months before his death, at age ninety-three, his second wife, then only in her mid-twenties, complained of his insistence on finishing all projects set for that day. While she believed that this was admirable in principle, she felt that it did not take into consideration that "sometimes one doesn't have as much energy as they would like." Scores of men that he had employed over the years would have chorused assent. They also, however, appreciated that he never spared himself, nor asked them to do anything he would not do.

Charles Goodnight, 1866, about to make his first drive with Oliver Loving. Courtesy Panhandle-Plains Historical Museum, Canyon, Texas.

In preparation for this drive, Goodnight put together a chuck wagon to be drawn by twenty oxen and carry provisions for eighteen men for the estimated six-hundred-mile drive. Loving decided that their venture merited portraits and persuaded a reluctant Goodnight to have them made by a photographer in Weatherford, where they outfitted for the long haul. Goodnight also took the opportunity to spend some time with a local resident, Miss Dyer.

By June 6, 1866, they had their herd of two thousand underway. The drive was complicated by the mixed nature of the cattle. It was further inconvenienced by quite a few of the cows dropping calves along the way. These had to be killed as they could not keep up. That was an unpleasant task as their mothers would become distraught and require special attention for a few days to prevent them from trying to return to the place that they were forced to leave their calves.

The trail Goodnight and Loving followed was well known as far as the Horsehead Crossing of the Pecos. Army detachments, and forty-niners heading for California had used it, but it was best known for being the route of the southern branch of the Butterfield Mail. Twice a week, between September 1858 and March 1861, coaches carried mail and passengers on the expensive — $200 per passenger — and exhausting trip. The segment Goodnight and Loving followed passed two abandoned forts, Phantom Hill and Chadbourne, and forded several waterways before reaching the Middle Concho and following it for about forty miles to its headwaters.

For drovers like Goodnight and Loving the real ordeal began when they left the Middle Concho and headed for the Pecos. It was nearly a hundred miles of dry country — no grass and no water. The second day the herd began to suffer. That night the cattle were on their feet, moaning and bellowing, but the cowboys held them in place. Goodnight and Loving concluded that if they could not rest, the only option was to keep them moving, and they did, although cattle began to drop by the wayside. The third night they reached Castle Gap, a narrow trail a mile long through the mountains, a dozen miles from the Pecos. The drovers held the herd there until daybreak so that they would have plenty of daylight to get the cattle across the river.

As soon as it was light, Goodnight collected all the canteens from the men and rode rapidly for the river. By the time he got back the herd had covered about half of the dozen miles to the Pecos. At that point, they divided the herd, with Goodnight taking the strongest two-thirds, leaving the weakest animals for Loving to push along. Goodnight was particularly careful to keep the cattle some distance from a pool of alkaline water, but three cows from Loving's herd found it and drank, and died shortly after.

Goodnight's two-thirds of the cattle, without loss, reached the notorious Horsehead Crossing, so named because of skeleton heads hung in scrub bush along the Pecos at that point. The banks were steep, and the depth of the channel and the rate of flow could change in a few minutes. The area was littered with the skeletons of cattle and horses. When the weaker animals under Loving reached the river, they jumped in and many did not have the strength to climb out on the other side. Their loss was in addition to about three hundred head that died on the trail from the Middle Brazos.

With the survivors watered and rested, Goodnight and Loving turned north. As Goodnight remembered it over half a century later, they had no trail to follow, but had to pioneer one, and the legend of the Goodnight-Loving Trail was born. J. Evetts Haley, in his biography of Goodnight, provides a map, reproduced here, that depicts the trail that Goodnight purportedly opened. In fact, they followed a route already well established. There are records of at least two herds, totaling 3,200 steers, being driven from Palo Pinto County to Fort Sumner, west of Fort Stanton, in the fall of 1865. Robert K. Wylie, an employee of James Patterson, holder of a beef contract for Fort Sumner, is credited with bossing that herd. Such events must have been the subject of much discussion among cattlemen in Palo Pinto County. In short, when Goodnight and Loving started their drive up the Pecos to Fort Sumner the next year, they must have known that others had preceded them on that route.

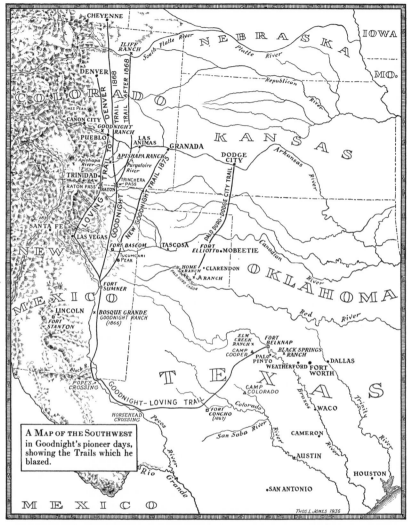

A MAP OF THE SOUTHWEST in Goodnight's pioneer days, showing the Trails which he blazed.

From J. Evetts Haley, *Charles Goodnight*, courtesy of the University of Oklahoma Press.

The only historian to directly address this conjecture is Charles Kenner in his *The Origins of the "Goodnight" Trail Reconsidered*. He points out that not until the 1930s was the trail from Horsehead Crossing to Fort Sumner labeled the Goodnight, or Goodnight-Loving Trail. Kenner credits J. Evetts Haley as being "primarily" responsible for crediting the opening of the trail to Goodnight and Loving. Undoubtedly, he was unaware of army correspondence documenting the herd driven up the trail in 1865 by James Patterson. Francis Mayhugh Holden has maintained that George T. Reynolds also delivered cattle to the fort in 1865.

Certainly the trail was not heavily traveled in 1866, and Goodnight and Loving found a ready market at the fort for the steers in their herd. They were paid eight cents a pound, on the hoof. J. Frank Dobie's estimate of an average weight of eight hundred pounds for longhorn steers would mean that Goodnight and Loving received about sixty-four dollars for animals worth no more than ten dollars back in Palo Pinto County. One can imagine how happy they were with their sale. And with the remaining 750 cows and calves, Loving would pioneer a trail north to Colorado, an area with which he had some acquaintance given his having driven cattle there in 1860. He sold the small herd to John Iliff, who had monopolized 150 miles of range along the South Platte.

Meanwhile, Goodnight's assignment was to convey their nearly twelve thousand dollars in gold back to Palo Pinto County, purchase a new herd, and drive it back to the Fort Sumner vicinity. He was accompanied on the trip back by four cowboys who had also made the trip over. On the Pecos River segment, Goodnight insisted that they travel only at night and hole up during the day, well off the trail. The gold was secured behind the mule that carried their grub.

But something that Goodnight could not have anticipated occurred. One night a storm, complete with lightning flashes and peals of thunder, stampeded the mule carrying the gold. It fled down the trail with Goodnight in pursuit. He finally was able to get ahead of the mule, jump from his mount and grab a rope trailing behind the runaway. The mule dragged him a considerable distance before it finally stopped. Goodnight was tremendously relieved to find that the gold was still attached to the back of the saddle — but their food was not. The only item they salvaged was a piece of bacon, but that could hardly subsist four active men very long. There was nothing to do but push on.

Not far from the Pecos crossing they encountered an apparition — a lone white man driving an ox-drawn wagon loaded with watermelons. This entrepreneur, with whom Goodnight was acquainted, was "Honey" Johnson, so-called because he also dealt in that commodity. He was bound for a salt lake where he hoped to sell his melons to Mexicans who regularly went there at this time for their annual supply of salt. Goodnight had to break the news to him that the word was that the Mexicans already had loaded their carts and departed. Thus, Johnson was more than happy to sell the Goodnight party all the melons that they could eat, and he also provided them sufficient provisions to make it to Fort Belknap.

Seventeen days after having left the Fort Sumner vicinity, Goodnight was back in Palo Duro County. There he put together a new herd of 1,200, restricting it to steers, after their unfortunate experience with cows on the first drive. And this time he required his hands to sign a statement that would govern their conduct on the trail — no drinking, gambling, or fighting. Anyone who violated the last ban, and in the fight killed his opponent, would be tried by the other hands and, if found guilty, summarily hanged. Rough-and-ready justice, indeed! The bans on drinking, gambling, and fighting would become customary features of every Goodnight drive and ranching operation, but the only penalty would be instant dismissal. In this practice he would not be alone among Panhandle ranchers.

This second drive was not without incident. It coincided with the annual southern migration of the buffalo, and the steers at one point mingled with a herd of buffalo bulls. It took some skillful and dangerous riding before the hands were able to round up all the steers.

Goodnight was able to innovate in one area and simplify

trailing. He noticed that one steer, early on, had established himself as the lead steer. Goodnight hung a bell around his neck, and, when ready to start in the morning, the steer's movement became the signal for the herd to rise and follow.

Having experienced the difficult stretch from the Middle Brazos to the Pecos, Goodnight this time kept the steers moving as much as possible. It worked, and he lost only five on the drive. And this time he held the herd at Bosque Redondo, about forty miles south of Fort Sumner. From that base he sold monthly to the army, and drove some cattle to the Santa Fe market. When Loving returned from Colorado, they settled in for the winter. During that layover they reached an oral agreement on a partnership in the cattle business.

The partnership got off to a rocky start. There was growing competition for the Fort Sumner business, and when spring came they still held about five hundred head. These they drove to pasture in the vicinity of Capulin Mountain in the northeast corner of New Mexico. Trouble with Mexican rustlers also had enlivened their layover. In one confrontation Goodnight ran down and killed a Mexican threatening to shoot him.

When spring came the partners prepared to return to the Upper Brazos for another herd. This trip, their gold — ten thousand dollars' worth — was carried in a wagon, and they had the reassurance of more guards. That proved to be fortuitous because Indians ambushed them before they reached Horsehead Crossing. But after a few volleys the Indians concluded that there were no easy pickings and retreated. Just to be on the safe side, Goodnight faked going into camp that evening, and after dark pushed down the trail to Horsehead, crossed it and headed for Castle Gap. There they met a herd headed for Fort Sumner and warned the owner of Indians ahead. He dismissed the danger, only to lose his entire herd to Indians as he approached Horsehead.

Goodnight and Loving made it back to the Upper Brazos and went to work putting a new herd together. Not surprising, they learned that the price of cattle had gone up, but got their herd together and headed back for Fort Sumner. This drive started off badly and turned worse. Indians were getting into the cattle business themselves, seizing herds on the trail and driving them to settlements in New Mexico to exchange for trade goods. Five years later, John Hittson, once sheriff of Palo Duro County, led a party of heavily armed Texans who reclaimed nearly six thousand of the stolen cattle. In the process, they shot up the village of Loma Parda, near Fort Union, and killed two of its citizens. The Texans did not distinguish between Mexican and Indian cattle thieves.

Goodnight had had more experience fighting Indians than had his partner. When they got underway on the Pecos trail to Fort Sumner, Loving became anxious about others beating them to the fort, where they had only an oral agreement with one contractor. Loving proposed that he go ahead and beat the competition. Goodnight tried to discourage him, but only got him to agree to take a companion — and travel at night. The companion would be One-Armed Bill Wilson, whom Goodnight believed to be "the coolest head in the outfit."

As Wilson remembered it thirty years later, the second day out, Loving ignored Goodnight's warning about daytime travel, and rode on. Not many miles later they spied Indians and immediately headed for the banks of the Pecos to find shelter. The warriors gradually overtook them, and, in the first exchange of gunfire, Loving was shot through the wrist, the round penetrating his side. Wilson managed to get him to the river, where they holed up under a bank, but the Indians knew their approximate location and closed in. One was crawling toward them, under cover of some reeds, only to encounter a rattlesnake that frightened him away. The Indians, however, maintained their perimeter, occasionally sending a shower of arrows to keep the white men in place.

When night fell, Loving persuaded Wilson that they should try to take advantage of the darkness and seek help. Loving believed that his wound was probably fatal, and he could only encumber Wilson and get both of them killed. Wilson reluctantly agreed and left his revolvers with Loving, but took his rifle. He removed his shoes and stripped to his long johns.

Wilson had not gone far downstream when he concluded that the rifle was too cumbersome, and he cached it against the bank. A hundred yards farther downstream, he encountered a mounted sentry. Wilson, however, was able to take advantage of some reeds and slipped by him. When he was well past the Indian, Wilson left the river and headed cross country to a point Goodnight and the herd should be passing soon.

For three days the barefoot Wilson was reminded that "everything in that country has stickers on it." His last night of this "painful journey," wolves followed him. Whenever he attempted to rest, they would awaken him, "snapping and snarling." When he reached the route the herd must follow, he found a "sort of cave," and waited until Goodnight and the cowboys came within hailing distance of the grotesque figure he presented.

Learning of Loving's plight, Goodnight quickly chose about a dozen men to accompany him and struck out for where Wilson said that he had left Loving. They located the spot, but no Loving, and concluded that the Indians had killed him. Later they encountered a party from Fort Sumner who informed him that Loving had escaped the Indians by emulating Wilson and had been picked up by some people who took him to the fort. When Goodnight reached it he found Loving alive, but suffering from a serious infection in the wounded arm. Fearing that it would spread, Goodnight demanded that the fort's physician amputate the arm. Unfortunately, this medic had never performed an amputation and was reluctant to proceed. By the time he finally agreed it was too late, and Loving died, September 25, 1867.

Before his death, Loving and Goodnight agreed that Goodnight would carry forward for two years their partnership in order to provide some financial security for Loving's family. His death was a real blow to Goodnight as he greatly admired the older man. Six decades later he declared, "I was so very fond of him, he was the nearest father to me I'd ever known. Gave me so much good advice on his death bed. . . . If I have any good qualities, I often thought that I owed them to that great man." He possibly would have found some consolation had he known that over a century later, Larry McMurtry, the prolific author of Western novels, would bring a version of the Goodnight-Loving odyssey to millions in *Lonesome Dove* and its screen adaptation.

As he lay dying, Loving extracted from Goodnight a promise to bury him back in Texas: "I don't want my bones to rest in alien soil." But first Goodnight had to drive to Colorado the cattle that he had been unable to sell in New Mexico. The trail lay through Raton Pass, where Dick Wooton, the old trapper, had made minor improvements and then imposed toll gates. Goodnight protested, but paid, and later opened a detour east of the pass and never again used Wooton's toll road. Goodnight chafed under any attempt to restrict his way of doing things.

On his return to Fort Sumner in October, Goodnight gladly fulfilled his promise to the dying Loving. He had the body exhumed and packed in charcoal in a casket that was slung on a wagon's running gear. In that fashion Loving was returned six hundred miles to a cemetery in Weatherford, where his family and friends interred him.

Goodnight then put together a herd of three thousand head and headed back to New Mexico. Indians made it a tough drive, harassing them repeatedly, and he had only 2,200 head when he reached the Bosque Redondo. After disposing of them he met Loving's son Joe, in Colorado, and together they worked to straighten out accounts for a final settlement. That would ultimately take place in Weatherford and involve bags of gold coin and gold dust, plus notes from debtors, all amounting to seventy-two thousand dollars, which was divided evenly between Goodnight's and Loving's heirs. Goodnight's generous handling of the settlement was the talk of Weatherford, whose population had known Goodnight in the years when he was just another struggling young cattleman. Now they recognized him for what he had become, a highly successful businessman with a remarkable record as cattle drover and Indian fighter.

While in Weatherford, Goodnight found time to court Mary Dyer. This must have been one of the longest courtships on the

Texas frontier, but each remained faithful. And Goodnight had reached the point where he was ready to give up driving cattle and turn to raising them on his own ranch to which he could bring a bride.

But first he must wind up the profitable relationship he had developed with John Simpson Chisholm, one of the most active dealers in cattle in Texas and New Mexico. He had begun his cattle operations in Denton County, north of Fort Worth, but during the Civil War had pushed farther west, by 1867 driving a herd to the Fort Sumner market. There he later encountered Charles Goodnight, and the two entered into a contract providing that Chisholm would have cattle driven to the Bosque Redondo area, where Goodnight would take over and drive them north to sell in Kansas, Colorado, or Wyoming; they would divide the profit. That arrangement lasted three years.

On one of the drives north, Goodnight established a ranch on the Arkansas River, a few miles west of Pueblo, to be known as the Rock Creek Bridge Ranch. With his usual volcanic energy he threw himself into putting together a model operation. This one would have not rail but stone corrals, also a stone barn, and an adobe house. But it would be not just a house but a home. He and Mary became engaged after a five-year courtship, which must have set a record for longevity in an area in which courtships were usually measured in months. She was the only woman to whom he was attracted, and she saw in him qualities that enabled her to overcome his preoccupation with his work, his brusque manner, and his vivid profanity.

But she did qualify her promise to marry him. The ceremony must take place in Hickman, Kentucky, where she had relatives. Moreover, once they were wed, her three younger brothers must live with them. Goodnight accepted her terms, but it would be a year before they were married.

When he did travel to his wedding, Goodnight detoured to Black Springs to see his mother. Over his protests, she insisted on washing and ironing all of his clothes. He then rode horseback to Galveston, where he boarded a steamboat to reach New

Mary Goodnight, ca. 1870, an able and self-reliant individual. Courtesy Panhandle-Plains Historical Museum, Canyon, Texas.

Orleans, there taking passage for the final leg to Hickman. They were wed July 26, 1870, and then departed for Colorado, accompanied by her brothers.

Mary had a difficult transition to life in Colorado. The last segment of the trip was by stagecoach from Abilene, Kansas, to Pueblo. It was distressingly long and uncomfortable, and the young bride arrived tired and depressed. And it would get worse. That first night in the village, vigilantes hanged three rustlers from a telegraph pole near the Goodnights' hotel. When Mary heard of it she demanded an explanation of the brutal frontier concept of justice. Her husband, confused by her anger, could think of nothing better than, "Well, I don't think it hurt the telegraph pole." This only further enraged her, and she retorted bitterly, "I used to think I knew you in Texas, but you have been out here among the Yankees and Ruffians until I don't know whether I know you or not, and I want you to take me back to Texas, I won't live in such a country." Nevertheless, after she had recovered from the rigors of the trip, and had been introduced to some of Pueblo's ladies, she relented and settled into the demanding role of a rancher's wife.

Her husband had a meteoric rise in Colorado. He quickly developed the Rock Creek Bridge property into a model operation, buying Durham bulls to upgrade his herd, planting the first orchard in the area, and harvesting the first irrigated crops in that part of the territory. With the capital he had amassed as a drover, Goodnight speculated in Pueblo real estate, buying town lots and even becoming part owner of the opera house. Enough of his money was invested in the new Stock Growers Bank of Pueblo that, despite his functional illiteracy, he became the head of the institution. The locals recognized his new status by conferring on him the title Colonel, by which some people would address him for the rest of his life.

Joseph G. McCoy, the man most instrumental after the Civil War in attracting a flood of Texas longhorns to Kansas cow towns, and the author of *Historic Sketches of the Cattle Trade of the West and Southwest,* described Goodnight in 1872 as a cattleman "having no superiors in the great new west." McCoy went on to declare that in two years Goodnight's ranching operation had made a profit of over 37 percent, an illustration of "the profitableness of stock-growing in southeastern Colorado."

But Goodnight's prosperity was ephemeral. A severe winter, followed by a drought, and then the Panic of 1873 that drove down beef prices combined to devastate the local economy, and he suffered severe losses. His cattle holdings were reduced to a herd of about 1,600, and he even shared ownership of them with brother-in-law Leigh Dyer and two young Englishmen who had come west to earn their fortunes. Casting about for another ranching possibility, Goodnight considered the Texas Panhandle, the last large area of Texas unpopulated by white men, due to its being a hunting ground for the Comanches and Kiowas. The Red River War of 1874–1875, however, was underway. Goodnight and other Texas and Colorado ranchers eyeing the Panhandle's millions of acres of grass would have to restrain themselves until the army had driven those tribes onto reservations in what would become Oklahoma.

Meanwhile, Goodnight drove the cattle that he co-owned southeast from Pueblo, with extended layovers along the way. During the winter of 1875–1876 the herd wintered on the Canadian River in eastern New Mexico. By that time the Red River War had ended, and the Indian barrier to settlement of the Texas Panhandle had been breached. Goodnight ordered his hands to drift the cattle into the Panhandle and then hold them along a stream that emptied into the Canadian River.

A Mexican who knew the Panhandle as a result of expeditions there to capture mustangs intrigued Goodnight with tales of a very large canyon with all that a rancher needed—abundant grass, good water, and depth sufficient to provide protection from wintry blasts. Goodnight persuaded the Mexican to guide him, and they set off to find the canyon. They rode too far east before turning south, but they finally found the Palo Duro as they worked their way back to the northwest. A cursory examination convinced Goodnight that the canyon was indeed all that he sought in a ranch, that he had found a home. Returning to the herd he prepared to make the move by accumulating supplies for six months, and by dispatching Leigh Dyer and a Mexican guide to locate a more-direct route. But first he needed to reach an understanding with sheepmen from New Mexico who also were migrating east, seeking new pasture for their animals.

Like cattlemen generally, Goodnight was convinced that cattle and sheep were incompatible, the wooly creatures seriously depleting pastures by cropping grass so short that they tore out the roots, virtually denuding the land. Moreover, energetic and overly zealous cowhands already had caused a crisis. Ordered by Goodnight to keep sheep out of contact with his cattle, they had run five hundred sheep into a boggy creek, where they drowned. Within weeks, a deputy from a New Mexico court had appeared with an order for one of the sheep killers to appear before a Las Vegas judge. It eventually resulted in Goodnight having to compensate the sheep's owner.

Anxious to avoid further problems with sheepmen, Goodnight reached an agreement with them. They would confine their activities to the Canadian River Valley, and he would keep his cattle farther south. Unfortunately for the sheepmen, other cattlemen quickly followed Goodnight into the Panhandle, and within a few years the New Mexicans would be forced to retreat to that territory.

In the fall of 1876, Goodnight pointed his herd in the direction of Palo Duro County. His life in the Panhandle was about to begin.

CHAPTER 3

The Land Awaits

ALTHOUGH there is no reason to believe that he was aware of it, Charles Goodnight arrived in Palo Duro Canyon soon after the Texas Legislature created the boundaries for the twenty-six counties of the Panhandle. When that was done in August 1876 there were no permanent residents in the Panhandle, and the first county government (Wheeler) would not come into existence until April 1879. Meanwhile, county boundaries, so conspicuous on maps in the state capitol, had no significance for the Panhandle's scanty population, which had to go southwest two hundred miles to Henrietta, county seat of Clay County, on matters requiring court action.

The total area of the Panhandle is 25,610 square miles, slightly larger than the entire state of West Virginia. In 1876 those county lines on the maps in Austin gave no clue to the geography of the Panhandle. Only twenty-five years earlier, members of the ill-fated Texan-Santa Fe Expedition had had a devastating introduction to the area when they came up against the intimidating heights of the eastern escarpment of the Llano Estacado (Staked Plains.) Today if you are flying in the late afternoon at 30,000 feet, parallel to the Llano Estacado, the escarpment appears as a 175-mile-long smudge, as it also appears on Texas highway maps. Atop it is the largest flat area in the Western Hemisphere, comprising about three-quarters of the Panhandle.

During the Civil War, Goodnight had accompanied Texas Rangers into the eastern quarter of the Panhandle. His detachments had not ventured, however, beyond the approaches to the forbidding escarpment, and they had seen nothing of the

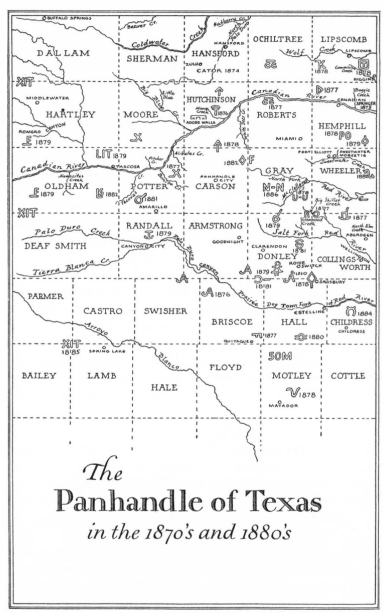

The
Panhandle of Texas
in the 1870's and 1880's

From Laura V. Hamner, *Short Grass and Longhorns,* courtesy of the
University of Oklahoma Press.

Staked Plains, the local name for the flat surface of the Llano. There have been numerous efforts to explain why the Llano was also called the Staked Plains. Goodnight was convinced that the designation derived from surveying stakes left behind by Captain John Pope's 1849 expedition seeking a railroad route to the Pacific along the 35th parallel. Possibly a better explanation is that the name derived from the practice of Indians on the treeless plains having to drive stakes to tether their most valuable horses.

Three centuries before Captain Pope ordered a subordinate to travel across the Llano to the headwaters of the Canadian, Spanish explorers had begun acquainting themselves with the region. In the eighteenth century the Comanches, together with the Kiowas with whom they shared a loose confederacy, began their domination by expelling Apache bands. During the same period Mexicans and Pueblo Indians began crisscrossing the area as *Comancheros* and *ciboleros*. The former took trade goods to locations in the eastern escarpment, where they met Southern Plains Indians and exchanged bread, hardware, powder, and the infrequent firearm, for the captives, buffalo hides, and meat of the tribesmen. The ciboleros also originated in the villages and pueblos of New Mexico, but these hardy hunters came to the plains intent on themselves killing the buffalo and carrying home cartloads of hides and meat. They traveled in parties large enough, hopefully, to discourage Indian attack. One result of this comanchero and cibolero activity was a number of trails and campsites they frequented annually, ample evidence that while American frontiersmen had a lot to learn about the Llano, its topography was no secret to inhabitants of New Mexico.

The first Spanish horsemen to encounter the Llano (even as today's motorist who travels by secondary roads across the plain for the first time) must have had some sense of discomfort, even foreboding, when confronted by an apparently limitless area with no object taller than a shrub as far as the eye could see. Nor were water sources obvious. Although the canyons that penetrated the eastern escarpment contained springs and creeks, these clefts in the Llano were difficult to detect from a distance on its flat surface. Nor were the numerous playas — very shallow ponds — apparent to the traveler until he was almost upon them. One army expedition crossing from west to east in 1849 thoughtfully left a stake on their trail to mark a playa nearby but undetectable at a distance. It is estimated that there were thousands of these ponds averaging several acres in size, but only in the rainy season did they fill, infrequent in an area with an average rainfall of only twenty-one inches in the eastern part of the Panhandle to seventeen in its western reaches. Due to the general aridity of the area and its strong winds, playas that might have two feet of water in them following a good rain, two weeks later would have lost it to evaporation and seepage through the surface.

It was not surprising then that the Llano Estacado inspired in its first American explorers feelings of unrest bordering on dread, and the belief that it held little promise for settlers. Lieutenant James W. Abert spent but one day on the Llano during his 1845 expedition, but in his diary he described it as "the day of anxiety." Finding no water, the expedition's members suffered from thirst while their fevered imaginations, stimulated by mirages, a common feature of travel on the plains, convinced them that they were being shadowed by Indians; "the wily savage had laid a play to decoy us upon this broad desert."

One of the most damning descriptions of the Llano was provided by another army officer, Captain Randolph B. Marcy, who commanded a military escort for forty-niners bound for California. In addition to protecting his charges, Marcy was ordered to report on the viability of the route from Fort Smith, Arkansas, to Santa Fe. Usually Marcy stayed in or near the Canadian River Valley, but for one day he detoured by way of the Llano, which he described in his final report:

> When we were upon the high table-land, a view presented itself as boundless as the ocean. Not a tree, shrub, or any other object, either animate or inanimate, relieved the dreary monotony of the prospect; it was a vast-illimitable expanse of

desert prairie — the dreaded "Lano Estacado" . . . the great Zahara of North America. It is a region almost as vast and trackless as the ocean — a land where no man, either savage or civilized, permanently abides . . . a treeless, desolate waste of uninhabitable solitude, which always has been, and must continue uninhabited forever.

Marcy also commented on the "very short buffalo grass" on "these barren plains," which animals avoided because of the insufficiency of water.

Three years later the army deputized Marcy to lead another expedition to discover the source of Red River. This time he approached the eastern escarpment from a point farther south than in 1849, and again he found it spectacular: "towering up some eight hundred feet above the surrounding country, and bordered by precipitous escarpments capped with a stratum of white gypsum which glistened like burnished silver."

In search of the source of Red River, Marcy explored a portion of Palo Duro Canyon, the largest in the eastern escarpment. But when confronted with a spring at the headwaters of one of its major tributary canyons, the Tule, he mistakenly termed it the source. He was guilty of an even greater error of judgment, concluding that the Llano, "in places two hundred miles wide, without a tree or running stream throughout its entire surface," was an "impassible barrier to a wagon road" and would "never be selected for a Pacific railway." Had he seen the herds of thousands of buffalo in their annual migrations, he might have recognized that the short grass in abundance was equally capable of sustaining large herds of cattle. But on the Llano he did not encounter a single buffalo and Lieutenant Abert, in his comparably brief exposure to the Llano, saw only two.

While Goodnight was ranching in Colorado, the soldiers and buffalo hunters were clearing the way for the arrival of settlers on the last frontier in Texas. The Red River War, 1874–1875, was precipitated in June 1874 by an Indian attack on the hated buffalo hunters at Adobe Walls in the Panhandle. The army's response was to send four converging columns into the Panhandle and the adjoining areas in northwest Texas. The most

aggressive of the commanders was Colonel Ranald S. Macken-
zie, whose operations included an attack on Comanche and
Cheyenne villages in the depths of Palo Duro Canyon. Although almost all of the Indians managed to escape their at-
tackers, they were forced to leave behind their tepees and other
possessions, which the troops destroyed. Even worse, the Indians lost about 1,500 horses, over a thousand of which Mac-
kenzie ordered slaughtered, denying the tribesmen the mobil-
ity so essential to their migratory way of life.

The buffalo hunters were the other threat to the Plains Indians, making serious inroads on their staff of life. The first
party had entered the Panhandle in 1873, ten men led by the
Mooar brothers. They, and the other hide hunters who would
follow them, were the motivation for merchants to establish
the trading post at Adobe Walls. Nor did the hunters retreat
from the area during the Red River War, despite a few of them
losing their scalps. Even more entered the killing spree after
the Indians had been driven onto reservations. In July 1881
Kiowas were elated to be able to track down just two buffalo, a
bull and a cow, the bull's head and skin being essential in their
Sun Dance ceremonies that summer. From that point on, only
a few buffalo held behind wire fences were left of the millions
that had roamed the South Plains.

The land was ready for the likes of Charles Goodnight, and in
the Palo Duro Canyon he had indeed found the most desirable
site in the Panhandle for a ranch. The main canyon was about
sixty-five miles long and described by Harley True Burton, in
his authoritative study of the JA Ranch, as "varied in width
from a half mile to over fifteen miles, and in depth from a few
hundred feet up to fifteen hundred. . . . On either side, every
few hundred yards a gully, ravine, or large creek, empties into
the canyon, each one of these gullies, ravines, or creeks is a
miniature canyon in itself several hundred feet deep." The major tributary canyons like the Tule and the Cita Blanco run for
miles before emptying into the Palo Duro.

Cattle require about fifteen gallons of water on summer days,
and the Palo Duro provided the best source in the Panhandle,

with the possible exception of some stretches of the Canadian River. The walls of the canyon and its tributaries also featured many springs that tapped the aquifers underlying the region. These springs provide clear, sweet water, a welcome relief from the gypsum-laden water so prominent in the accounts of explorers of the Panhandle. Good pasture grasses were relatively abundant. They included a combination of short grasses like blue grama and buffalo that prevailed on the Llano Estacado, some side oats and hairy grama, and little blue stem. In the canyons the higher-moisture-content soils produced good pasture and a variety of trees, including hackberry, mesquite, cedar, and cottonwood. Grapevines festooned trees, and plum bushes abounded. During favorable times of the year the cattle could be driven up to the Llano to graze, giving canyon pastures a chance to recuperate. Little wonder that Goodnight stated unequivocally, "I wanted that canyon." The next ten years of his life would be devoted to acquiring as much of it as he could buy or preempt.

CHAPTER 4

Into the Palo Duro

ONCE he concluded in late October that the Palo Duro Canyon indeed had all the natural features he sought for a ranch, Charles Goodnight and his men began to trail the herd, single file, down a steep path to the floor of the canyon. At that point the Palo Duro was relatively narrow. Goodnight quickly decided to drive the cattle farther down the canyon, as it gradually widened toward its mouth. The move, about fifteen miles in all, turned into an exciting buffalo drive as the riders encountered what Goodnight estimated to have been as many as ten thousand. He, his brother-in-law Leigh Dyer, and James T. Hughes, a young Englishman who owned a small interest in the cattle, led the charge down the canyon, occasionally firing their pistols at any buffalo that lingered. This added to the din of the stampede as the frightened animals charged through the underbrush and stirred up clouds of dust, and the thunder of their hooves echoed off the canyon walls.

According to Hughes, the son of the author of *Tom Brown's School Days,* who wrote two letters that were published in an English journal, Goodnight's first order of business was to establish the eastern boundary of his range and delegate a couple of his hands to keep the buffalo from returning. He then headed north to Colorado to obtain financing to properly stock his range and take care of other expenses until he could begin to market his cattle. Hughes described one difficult chore he had left to the hands, getting the wagons and their contents to safety on the canyon floor. As the middle third of the trail was quite precipitous, at that point the wagons had to be emptied and winched down backward, using ropes wrapped around trees to

slow their descent. The wagons' contents the men themselves
had to laboriously pack down the steep stretch.

Although the hands did not know it, only six months earlier
Lieutenant Ernest Ruffner's expedition to examine the head of
Red River encountered similar problems in getting their wagons to the floor of the canyon. The day before they had camped
on the Llano at the edge of one of the Palo Duro's tributary
canyons and their only water source at that site was at the
canyon's bottom. To reach it the men had to descend a slope so
steep that at points they had to sit down and slide. To carry
buckets of water up that miserable trail was "regular convict
labor," complained one member of the detachment.

In Goodnight's absence the men rode herd on the cattle and
constructed a dugout in the side of a bank, shoring up the walls
with local stone and stabilizing the roof with cottonwood and
cedar logs. (A reconstruction of what probably was that dugout can be seen today in Palo Duro State Park.) Meanwhile, the
hands did some hunting to supplement their scanty rations.
They were able to kill a few wild turkeys and two black bears.
The meat of the latter Hughes described as delicious. Their
boss also left them orders to begin construction of a house and
corrals.

That Goodnight had staked out his claim in the very nick of
time became apparent on January 5 when Hughes challenged
men scouting for an open range for their own cattle. In the
same period he observed a party of five buffalo hunters at their
grisly work. The young Englishman commented on the "fright-
ful waste of meat" and predicted that "the buffalo will be almost
a thing of the past in twenty years," badly underestimating the
killing ability of the hide hunters. The soldiers had smashed the
Indian barrier to settlement of the Panhandle, and the hunters
were rapidly clearing it of the buffalo so that Charles Goodnight and his fellow ranchers could monopolize the range.

Goodnight won the title of first rancher in the Panhandle by
a narrow margin. As nearly as can be determined, in early November 1876, Thomas Sherman Bugbee located a herd in the
breaks of the Canadian River, rough ground that provided his

1,800 head some protection from the harsh winter winds. A Maine Yankee and veteran of some of the worst battles of the Civil War, Bugbee migrated west after the war and entered the cattle business, operating a ranch in Kansas before moving to the Panhandle and establishing the Quarter Circle T. As Mary Goodnight had not yet reached the Palo Duro, Mary Catherine Bugbee had the distinction of being the first Anglo ranch wife to take up residence in the Panhandle. The Bugbees had one major problem that Goodnight was spared. The Palo Duro Canyon simplified the task of keeping buffalo off Goodnight's range, while Bugbee had to hire extra hands to prevent the shaggy beasts from mingling with his cattle.

Goodnight, however, could not match Bugbee's financial resources, as was demonstrated by his quick departure from Palo Duro in November 1876 to seek funding. Fortunately, bankers at Pueblo promptly advanced their former colleague necessary letters of credit addressed to post traders at Fort Dodge in Kansas, Fort Supply in Oklahoma, and Fort Elliott, newly erected in the eastern Panhandle, about seventy-five miles northeast of the Palo Duro.

In February 1877 Goodnight returned to the canyon by a roundabout route, traveling by rail from Trinidad to Dodge City and from there to Fort Supply by government coach. As army officers took all the seats from there to Fort Elliott, he was forced to hire a guide at Fort Supply for the over-two-hundred-mile horseback ride to the Palo Duro. Snow was on the ground and the wind bitterly cold, but otherwise the trip was uneventful until they reached a tributary of the Canadian in the Panhandle. Here, some rough characters were encamped, the band of outlaws led by Henry Boren, better known as Dutch Henry. He was a former buffalo hunter who had been at Adobe Walls when the Indians attacked in June 1874. As the buffalo diminished rapidly, Dutch Henry had shifted to the roles of cattle rustler and highwayman.

As Goodnight remembered it fifty years later, his guide wanted to slip past the gang under the cover of darkness, but the rancher insisted on meeting Dutch Henry. Entering the lion's den, Goodnight asked for their leader, and when the personable young man stepped forward, he made him a proposition. If the outlaw stayed away from the Palo Duro, Goodnight would not interfere with what the gang did farther north. To make his proposition more credible, the rancher referred to his "bunch of good men, well armed and good shots." To his considerable relief Dutch Henry replied, "Well, old man, you are D— plain about it, but it is a fair proposition and I will do it." Considerably relieved, Goodnight sealed the bargain by hauling from his saddlebags a bottle of French brandy for drinks all around. His blunt, direct approach had done the job; Dutch Henry might be a problem elsewhere, but the ranch in the Palo Duro was spared his attention.

Reassured that the cattle were making it through the winter in good shape and that the cowboys were tending to their chores, Goodnight hurried back north to meet his wife, whom he had persuaded to visit relatives in California while he was finding their new home in the Panhandle. Mary had tired of this arrangement and notified him that she would be arriving in Denver at a certain time and expected him to meet her. He narrowly met the deadline, riding hard to Trinidad, where he caught a train that got him to Denver just in time to meet Mary's.

While in Denver he managed to borrow thirty thousand dollars using his remaining property near Pueblo as security. The rate was a usurious 18 percent a year, but the agent brought him into contact with the source of the money. This was John George Adair, an Irish financier, who had discovered that he could borrow money in the British Isles and lend it in the United States at a substantially higher rate. In New York he had opened a place of business, which he subsequently moved to Denver. Not content to just lend to ranchers, Adair had decided to engage in the business himself — if he could find someone sufficiently experienced to manage his property. After interviewing Goodnight, who came highly recommended, Adair had his attorney draw up a contract, which the two men signed June 18, 1877.

John George Adair, an Irish landlord with money to invest in Texas land. Courtesy Panhandle-Plains Historical Museum, Canyon, Texas.

The contract provided Adair ample safeguard for his investment, but proved a profitable deal for Goodnight as well. The
Irishman would provide the financial backing for a ranching
venture that Goodnight would manage, at an annual salary of
$2,500, plus a one-third interest in the operation. Adair ad-
vanced him the money necessary for his one-third interest as a
loan at 10 percent interest. Adair protected his investment by
specifying that Goodnight would devote his full energies to the
position and not sign or endorse any notes that might compro-
mise him financially. In addition, Adair would be guaranteed
an overall 10 percent return on his investment.

The terms of Adair's initial investment were clearly deline-
ated. He would advance all the necessary capital, within certain
specified parameters. No more than twenty-five thousand acres
would be acquired, and the herd would not be permitted to
exceed fifteen thousand head, a number that indicated that substantially more land would be grazed than paid for in an environment where one cow per ten acres was an optimistic estimate. The contract would run for five years, and the cattle
would carry the brand JA, an arrangement of Adair's initials.

Goodnight was delighted with the contract. It would pay
him well, and he would be able to put together the type of
ranching operation that he had dreamed of but could not fi-
nance on his own. Adair, for his part, had managed to retain an
individual acknowledged by his peers as a superior rancher
with a vision of the ideal cattle operation and the drive and skill
to bring it to fruition.

It would never be, however, a comfortable personal relationship. Adair epitomized the highborn Irish gentleman whose
firmly held views of class relationships ill fitted him to deal with
a highly democratic Panhandle society. Indeed, Adair had been
roundly denounced even in Ireland, in 1861, for reacting to the
murder of the steward of one of his estates by evicting forty-
seven tenant families and razing their homes. Many of the
younger evictees could do no better than migrate to far-distant
Australia, supported by a fund raised by other outraged Irish-
men. Most of the older victims ended up in poorhouses, or

became homeless vagabonds. Even in an Ireland noted for landlords who abused their tenants, Adair was notorious.

Goodnight resented Adair's air of superiority and, in his old age, remembered the Irishman as "an overbearing old devil." He regretted that on one occasion, when Adair was being particularly obnoxious, that he had not pulled him from his saddle and given him a sound thrashing. Like other upper-class Englishmen who appeared in the American West in the late nineteenth century, Adair had a concept of employer-employee relations alien to American cowboys. One cowboy on the Northern Plains supposedly responded to a question from an Englishman as to where his "master" was with a belligerent, "The son-of-a-bitch ain't been born yet!"

Adair was very unpopular with the JA hands. He earned their grudging respect, however, on one occasion. He had appeared one morning with a peremptory order to saddle a horse for him. The cowboy to whom the order had been given selected a bronco that usually could be counted upon to buck when first mounted. The conspirator and a few of the other cowhands took up unobtrusive positions and prepared to witness the humiliation of this objectionable owner. To their surprise and chagrin the bronco submitted peacefully to Adair mounting him and then walked off on command as if he had never bucked in his life.

Both Adair and his wife, Cornelia, had reputations as excellent riders, despite his embarrassing misadventure in 1874, on his only buffalo hunt. He shot his horse in the head while chasing a herd across the prairie. Cornelia Adair had been born into the baronial Wadsworth family in upstate New York and knew farming and stock raising as practiced in the Genesee Valley. As a member of the American landed gentry she had had ample experience dealing with tenants and field hands — men who would not submit to the treatment accorded their British counterparts. She demonstrated her credentials as a rider to Goodnight when she rode the entire four hundred miles from Trinidad to the Palo Duro, and when they arrived he could not find a blemish on her horse's back. Meanwhile, Mary Good-

Cornelia Adair, member of an upstate New York family with large landholdings. Courtesy Panhandle-Plains Historical Museum, Canyon, Texas.

night had been driving a wagon that her husband had rebuilt. It was definitely better sprung than an ordinary wagon and had a heavy-duty canvas top with extra tie-downs to combat those strong Llano winds.

The ride from Trinidad to the Palo Duro occurred in July 1877, after Goodnight had assembled four wagonloads of equipment and supplies needed for the ranch. He also purchased, with funds advanced by Adair, one hundred purebred Durham bulls. Already Goodnight was thinking of ways to upgrade the quality of JA cattle.

The trip over was not without its tense moments. Goodnight constantly scouted ahead to locate the water holes so scarce once they reached the Llano Estacado. This was in the same month that, some fifty miles southwest of Palo Duro Canyon, four black troopers of a detachment of the Tenth Cavalry, in pursuit of Comanches, died of thirst when they lost their way on the boundless plain. On one occasion when Goodnight was scouring the country ahead for desperately needed water, he left Mary with instructions to follow in the general direction he had headed. He was hardly out of sight when an Indian sighting frightened Mary into circling the wagons and preparing for attack. When he did find water, Goodnight retraced his route, expecting to find Mary and the Adairs well along the trail. Instead he found them corralled and immobilized by fear, not far from where he had left them. He quickly concluded that what Mary and the cowboy who had raised the first alarm identified as Indians were actually tufts of grass transformed into warriors' headdresses by the mirage effect so common on the high plains.

Nevertheless, the possibility of Indian attack was sufficiently credible that army high command had ordered the commandant of the nearest post, Fort Elliott, to provide the Adairs a military escort that met them before the small wagon train had reached the Palo Duro. Cornelia was well connected with the army. Her father, a Civil War major general, had been killed at the Battle of the Wilderness in 1864, and her three brothers and her first husband had also served as officers in the Union Army.

The Adairs remained in the Palo Duro for only a brief period, and that would be one of the only two visits that John Adair ever made to the ranch. Given his dislike for the man, Goodnight did not miss him, and he now had the financial backing he had sought. He had insisted that Adair commit to buying land for the ranch, as opposed to just preempting it. That had led to the clause in their contract providing for the purchase of no more than twenty-five thousand acres, and the Irishman would not agree to buying more than twelve thousand acres the first year.

But Goodnight soon learned that there were other serious obstacles to their occupying the canyon. It had been surveyed and claimed by Jot Gunter and his partner William B. Munson. The two were land speculators who had purchased state land certificates in early 1870, when Texas was in serious financial straits and desperate to find a way to pay for internal improvements, principally railroads. One scheme was to issue certificates, each worth 640 acres of the public domain, which in Texas belonged to the state, as a result of the terms of the annexation agreement of 1845. The certificates were assigned railroad companies, which in turn sold them to land speculators such as Gunter and Munson, for the equivalent of about twenty-five cents per acre.

Beginning in 1874 Gunter and Munson kept surveying parties out ahead of settlement, locating land in the Panhandle, including the Palo Duro. Thus when Goodnight finally had the money to buy the canyon, most of it had been surveyed and claimed by the speculators. Gunter and Munson, however, had never intended to develop the land themselves, but rather to sell it at a profit to ranchers such as Goodnight and Adair. The speculators soon discovered that Goodnight could drive a sharp bargain.

He was up against Adair's limitation of no more than twelve thousand acres being purchased in the first year of the JA Ranch, but Goodnight had a strategy to enable them to acquire most of the canyon, using what Goodnight liked to refer to as the "old crazy quilt" process of selection. Gunter, with whom he dealt, demanded $1.25 per acre, but Goodnight finally got him down to seventy-five cents — and would pay that only if Goodnight could choose individual parcels to make up the total twelve thousand acres. He got this stipulation written into the contract, and then held Gunter, who soon recognized that he had been outfoxed, to those terms.

With this latitude, Goodnight later gloated, "I took all the good land and all the water I could get, and under the contract they were to let me designate 12,000 more that I was to take the next year at my option. Well, I scattered that all over the Palo Duro Canyon. . . . Every place a man was liable to come, I took." It was a real coup. Goodnight had made it very difficult for another rancher to find sufficient water and good pasture in the Palo Duro to support a large herd. The parcels the JA now had title to, however, were interspersed among school lands, alternate 640-acre sections reserved to support public education. Since these sections were also grazed by JA cattle, the ranch at the end of 1878 encompassed nearly fifty thousand acres. The lack of title to about half the ranch guaranteed trouble down the road. But that was only one of the problems facing Goodnight as he struggled to turn the JA into the ranch of his dreams.

CHAPTER 5

Launching the JA Ranch, 1877–1880

FOLLOWING the signing of the first contract between Charles Goodnight and John George Adair, the Texan worked like a man possessed to realize his dream of developing the best ranch possible. This required attention to a multiplicity of details, from acquiring land and cattle to determining how to lay out the pastures to maximize utilization of grass and water resources. Goodnight strove constantly to develop the best breed of cattle that would both cope with the conditions peculiar to the Panhandle and reproduce at a good rate and command the best prices at Dodge City and Kansas City stockyards. Last but not least, to realize his dreams Goodnight had to recruit and retain employees who would meet his rigorous standards.

Nor was he alone in these aspirations. Between 1876 and 1880 nearly twenty other large ranches of 100,000 acres or more appeared in the Panhandle. The founders of these properties were slow to follow the example of Goodnight and Adair and purchase land. With the help of loans from a Scottish firm, the Texas Land and Mortgage Company, the JA continued to expand, and totaled 93,679 acres by 1882. The impetus for this company came from an Englishman, Arthur Renshaw, who had visited the JA in company with the Adairs, and had talked with Goodnight about the Panhandle's economic prospects. W. S. Kerr, author of the standard account of the company, declared: "While there is little doubt that the Adairs influenced Renshaw personally, Goodnight's commanding knowledge of the area and its opportunities clinched the decision." Renshaw was one of many who would recognize Goodnight's expertise, a resource the Texan generously shared with all comers.

That Adair was an early member of the board of the Texas Land and Mortgage Company undoubtedly facilitated its several loans, totaling about $300,000. The loans carried an interest rate of about 12 percent and, as partners, both Adair and Goodnight were required to sign the mortgages. Over time, the knowledge of the size of the indebtedness became a serious concern to Goodnight. Adair, who was constantly buying properties in Ireland and England and then mortgaging them to buy more, apparently found these financial burdens less stressful. Goodnight, however, did enjoy the wheeling and dealing involved in the actual purchase of land at prices ranging from twenty to thirty-five cents per acre.

One thing that Goodnight did not enjoy as he expanded the JA land holdings was his infrequent encounters with the former lords of the Southern Plains, the Comanche Indians and their allies, the Kiowas and Plains Apaches. For several years after the Red River War, bands of these Indians slipped away from their reservations in western Oklahoma in search of game. The size of the rations the government issued them, approximately half that allotted soldiers, was based on the assumption that they would partially support themselves by hunting while converting to farming and stock raising. Most of the reservations' game was quickly killed off, and in 1876 Congress prohibited Indians from crossing Red River into Texas to hunt. Texas Rangers took this as license to kill any Indians found south of the river, or in the Panhandle. Nevertheless, small parties continued to escape from the reservations to hunt. Frantic agents, caught between starving and desperate Indians and harsh federal policy, sometimes were able to arrange with Fort Sill to provide military escort for hunting parties.

As the man presiding over one of the largest properties on the Indians' old hunting grounds, Charles Goodnight inevitably was faced with this potentially dangerous problem. In January 1879, bands totaling about three hundred Comanches and Kiowas were hunting buffalo. Finding none, and on the verge of starvation, they began killing JA cattle. As Goodnight remembered it in the 1920s, after learning of the depredations he sought out the band and asked Quanah Parker, a Comanche chief, to accompany him to ranch headquarters to discuss the situation. There they reached an agreement by which the Indians pledged to stop killing cattle and in return Goodnight would give them two steers every other day until arrangements could be made for their return to the reservation. The rancher later billed the government for thirteen head of cattle at twenty-five dollars per head.

Late in Goodnight's life, well after Quanah had attained the status of a regional celebrity, the rancher described what had occurred as making a "treaty," during the negotiation of which Goodnight had posed as a Coloradan because of the intensity of the Indians' hatred and fear of Texans. He also sometimes referred to having "captured" Quanah. That was an exaggeration, as during the several weeks they were in the area, the Indians were accompanied by troops, first from Fort Sill, and when that detachment was withdrawn, by troopers from Fort Elliott, whose commander Goodnight had advised of the problem.

Although Goodnight's memory of the encounters was probably no more accurate than that of anyone trying to recall events nearly half a century old, he had generally conducted himself admirably in this and subsequent contacts with the Indians. What made this remarkable was that he had personally fought Indians and suffered grievously at their hands. To the end of his days he continued to revere the memory of Oliver Loving, whom Comanches were presumed to have killed. Moreover, in the 1870s, Goodnight had attempted unsuccessfully to obtain reimbursement from New Mexican courts for the loss of thousands of cattle that Plains Indians stole from him and traded to Comancheros, who in turn sold them to New Mexican ranchers. As late as the 1890s, Goodnight filed suit in the Federal Court of Claims in an only-partially successful effort to secure compensation for his losses.

The last recorded Comanchero expedition to the Plains occurred in 1880. Nevertheless, their old trading partners continued to leave the reservation to visit their traditional camping sites in the western escarpment of the Llano Estacado. Over the years, a few Indians would call on Goodnight and enjoy his hospitality as they sat around a campfire and traded old war stories from a shared past. Inevitably, these accounts were somewhat embellished, but Goodnight played along, recognizing that the ex-warriors had little left but memories of their glory days on the Plains. Now they honored their onetime antagonist while enjoying his hospitality. And Goodnight sold a buffalo to the Kiowas, who in 1887 sought the head of a buffalo bull to properly perform their annual Sun Dance ceremony. A year later he was still trying to get the fifty dollars the Indians had agreed to pay.

Other Panhandle white settlers had their own memories. As late as 1890, the entire area was panicked by a quickly spreading rumor — Indians were on the warpath! At the JA and other ranches people prepared to defend themselves. At the village of Clarendon, about twenty miles from JA headquarters, frightened citizens broke into a hardware store and seized arms and ammunition worth three hundred dollars for which the proprietor was never compensated. One of the railroads, which by that time had entered the Panhandle, carried a trainload of volunteers from communities to the east. Armed to the teeth, and overly fortified by whiskey consumed en route, when the volunteers reached Clarendon some of them had difficulty getting off the train.

With the fear of Indian attack not far beneath the surface as late as 1890, it is little wonder that in the early days of the JA Mary Goodnight was reluctant to remain alone at the Old Home Place. This was initially only a three-room log cabin that her husband threw together some distance down the canyon from the dugout that was the first ranch headquarters. With no other women within forty miles, she was happy to have the companionship of three chickens, which she made pets of after one of the ranch hands surprised her with them. In those first years, she frequently chose to join her husband on his travels around the ranch to check on the stock and how his cowhands were discharging their duties. She even accompanied him when he drove herds to Dodge City.

On all these occasions, Mary rode a sidesaddle that her husband had designed especially for her. He was proud of his accomplishment and years later, when he donated it to the Panhandle-Plains Historical Museum, noted that it had won a prize when exhibited at a fair in England. Goodnight also fondly remembered Patty, Mary's mount from that period — handsome, well gaited, and fast. The horse was very attached to Mary — or the treats she provided — and when she chose to ride in her wagon for a time, Patty would stride along with the wagon and come to her mistress when called.

Goodnight's cattle drives had in the late 1860s and early 1870s been efficiently organized and conducted, and his ranch near Pueblo had been a model operation, so it comes as no surprise that those qualities would be exhibited in the JA. He was discriminating in his hiring, as was revealed in one oft-repeated account of the experience of a teenager who sought employment by Goodnight. Like many other young ranch recruits, he was a "nester kid," a poor farm boy to whom ranch life probably seemed glamorous when compared to the deadly monotony of life on a pioneer homestead. Certainly it was not the roughly thirty dollars a month, monotonous meals featuring beef and beans, and rude housing that attracted the applicants.

Goodnight's qualifying exam for a job applicant could be to dig and chop until he had removed all the mesquite roots — notoriously tough and wide-ranging — from a designated plot of land. The rancher would be sure that the plot was large enough to defeat all but the most dedicated and tireless workers. As for the fine points of cowboying, the youth could learn these from his fellow ranch hands and Goodnight.

The rancher had had strict rules for his employees when he was driving cattle to Fort Sumner and points north. On one drive he fired all his hands for gambling and continued alone to the not-too-distant objective. He also ran a tight ship as ranch owner and manager, although he never went so far as one superintendent of the XIT Ranch, who codified twenty-three

"General Rules" to dictate the conduct of his hands. Goodnight would not tolerate gambling, drinking, or fighting. Violation of those rules could mean instant dismissal.

It was not a matter of morality with Goodnight — he enjoyed a toddy — but the inexcusable waste of time and energy. Even the sight of his men playing mumblety-peg could bring down upon them a storm of profanity. And abuse of horses was a serious offense in the rancher's eyes. Untoward use of spurs, failure to loosen the saddle girth when dismounting for an extended time, even having a filthy saddle blanket when conditions made it possible to wash it, could bring down on the head of the culprit his strongly worded displeasure.

Goodnight's employees always knew, however, that their boss was himself not afraid of work. Indeed, they preferred that he not join them in a task because he could forget lunch and rest periods, and they dared not break on their own. Whatever was being done, he thought that he was able to do it better than his hands, and usually could. One friend was surprised to drop in at JA headquarters to find Goodnight shoeing mules while the blacksmith, to whom he was paying the handsome salary of $150 a month, shooed flies from the animal being worked on.

Charles Goodnight might be a stern taskmaster, but he respected his men. Since his youth he had worked cattle, and he continued to be intimately involved in all phases of ranch operation. And, unlike most owners and managers of ranches in the last quarter of the nineteenth century, he had shared with his men the terror of Indian attacks, a real bonding experience. He had little in common with people like John Clay, a Scot who was an authority on financial management of ranches, but had never experienced the dangers and physical demands of a cattle drive through hostile Indian country. Clay once described cowboys as "the chief obstacle of the range . . . mostly illiterate, uncivilized; who drank and thieved and misbranded cattle." Goodnight saw cowhands through a different prism: "I wish I could find words to express the trueness, the bravery, the hardihood, the sense of honor, the loyalty to their trust and to each other."

Goodnight was a white Texan, and never forgot it, but he recognized merit in whatever color it came, as witnessed by his relationship with Bose Ikard, an ex-slave. Ikard had been an employee of Goodnight's mentor, Oliver Loving. After his death, for several years Ikard worked for Goodnight. But when the rancher settled near Pueblo, he advised Ikard that Colorado was even less hospitable than Texas to African Americans; Ikard returned to Texas, dying in Henrietta on January 4, 1929. Goodnight's advice was probably sound. A few years after Ikard left Colorado a Pueblo orator completed a talk to a local audience with the following lines:

Here the wild Indian once roamed
Fished, fit and bled.
Now the inhabitants are white
With nary red.

Goodnight and Ikard kept in touch frequently, and his old boss would on occasion give Ikard a little financial help. Early in 1929 Goodnight responded to inquiries about Ikard from his biographer, J. Evetts Haley, with the suggestion that Haley get in touch with Ikard: "He was a wonderful rider and no man was more reliable. . . . I feel under more obligations to John Rumans [another former employee] and Boaz [*sic*] Ikard than any living man and if I was a millionaire I would have them both on pension." When Goodnight inquired about Ikard he learned of his recent death. As he wrote Haley, "This now leaves me the only surviving member of the party of 18 who laid off the Goodnight and Loving trail in 1866. Negro though he was, his death affects me greatly. He was a man of remarkable morals, hadn't a single bad habit and was surely true and faithful to me. He participated in three different Indian skirmishes with me, no better night rider ever saddled a horse." Goodnight later ordered a granite marker for Ikard's grave with the following inscription: "Served with me four years on the Goodnight-Loving trail, never shirked a duty or disobeyed an order, rode with me in many stampedes, participated in three engagements with Comanches. Splendid behavior. Goodnight."

That was probably more praise than Ikard would have heard from Goodnight over the years that he worked for the man. Although capable of volcanic eruptions when angered, the rancher was normally closemouthed. A story told about how he chose to rebuke men putting in fence posts illustrates this side of the legendary figure. The men first observed their boss riding up the line of posts they had emplaced, then dismounting to easily uproot several posts. Having made his point, Goodnight rode back the way he had come without ever approaching the men, or even acknowledging their existence. But they had gotten the message and began planting the posts deeper, as was expected in a "Goodnight fence."

He could be equally sparing in his praise. Bones, a black man whose specialty was breaking horses, had spent considerable time training a horse to perform tricks. He finally mustered enough nerve to ask Goodnight to come to the door of ranch headquarters and observe while he put the horse through his repertoire. After a flawless performance, all that the trainer received was a summary grunt from his boss, who turned on his heel and went back to work. Probably Bones was relieved that Goodnight did not tongue-lash him for having wasted valuable time on something that added nothing to the ranch's bottom line.

The part-owner and manager of the JA needed the best from his men as he worked to realize his idea of a model cattle operation. Improving the quality of its stock was a top priority. Longhorns, like those Goodnight had driven out of Texas by the thousands, were the foundation of the original JA herds. Already the old Spanish strain had been altered by the introduction of English breeds, which resulted in a hybrid that was a somewhat better beef producer but that retained the long legs that enabled the longhorn to graze farther from water and cover ground more rapidly on the trail to market. They also had the longhorns' ability to forage for themselves and protect their young from most predators. But at the end of the drive to market they did not have the quantity and quality of beef the packing houses preferred. Longhorns provided only lean, stringy beef, what was referred to in the East as "cheap meat for poor folks." And the considerable breadth of their horns, their hallmark, was a definite disadvantage when moving them by rail as fewer head could be crammed into the cars. It is ironic that today a portion of the old JA supports the Double Helix, a ranch specializing in longhorns. One of their selling points is their "long, spectacular horns." Another is their "leaner and healthier" meat, no longer cheap meat for poor folks.

What Goodnight and all other ranchers sought to do was to breed an animal that would flourish in the plains environment and produce more and better beef. His first venture into selective breeding was on his ranch near Pueblo when he invested three thousand dollars in Durham bulls. When he moved the herd to the Panhandle it included about 150 Durham cows and a thoroughbred bull of one of the best Durham strains. By crossing the longhorn with the Durham, Goodnight hoped to produce an animal as good a forager as the longhorn but substantially larger. The results were indeed gratifying. By one estimate, a three-and-a-half-year-old longhorn steer might weigh 825 pounds, but the cross would tip the scales at an impressive 1,100. The first Adair money that Goodnight spent on cattle purchased a hundred Durham bulls, which the Goodnight-Adair party drove to the Palo Duro after the partnership was formed. Within a few years, however, Goodnight would conclude that although the longhorn-Durham breed was a distinct improvement, that other crosses might offer even more.

But the Panhandle rancher had other concerns, such as contending with the prairie dogs that ate grass in competition with his cattle, and predators such as wolves, coyotes, and cougars, which could cut into his calf crop. Today the Great Plains Historical Museum in Lawton, Oklahoma, has a prairie dog town on its grounds, and the lively, attractive little animals are a delight to observe. To the ranchers they were a squalid and expensive nuisance. Their towns could cover hundreds of acres, and a large one could have over a thousand occupants, each eating the short grasses that otherwise could be fattening cattle. And their numbers multiplied as their predators, coyotes in particular, were hunted down because of their own threat to the cattle.

Charles Goodnight ranked eliminating prairie dogs pretty low in his priorities when he moved into the Palo Duro, but in the fall of 1877 he hired a professional hunter to rid his range of any remaining buffalo and predators. In the latter category the lobo wolf, with its ravenous appetite for red meat, was the principal problem. The lobo's primary source of meat became calves, but when operating in packs, they could cut yearlings and cows out of the herd. One lobo in the course of a year could kill up to seventy-five head. To deal with the problem Goodnight employed Gus Hartman, a professional hunter. The rancher would provide rations and poison and pay a bounty for each varmint for which the hunter and his sidekick, Rufe Lefors, a boy in his teens, could produce proof of kill.

In his old age Lefors wrote a memoir with the wonderful title *Facts as I Remember Them*. In it he recalled their experiences as bounty hunters in the fall and winter of 1877–1878. They killed buffalo and saved their hides. They sliced the meat and hung it to dry to make jerky that Goodnight had promised to buy at five cents per pound. Lefors does not specify the number of animals they shot or poisoned, but he remembered how happy the rancher was with the result, as were the hunters themselves, who had done "very well financially." The youth also had fond memories of Christmas 1877 because Molly Goodnight invited them to join the ranch hands for a celebration. She had decorated a tree and provided a present for everyone. LeFors remembered his as a "large, beautiful silk" neckerchief such as the cowboys sported on their rare visits to town.

Bounties were an answer to the predator population, but insects such as heel flies were a problem without an obvious solution. In the spring, swarms of these tiny, stinging insects attacked the cattle. In desperation they would run to creeks and stand in water or mud over their ankles. Sometimes they would become bogged down and die unless a cowboy lassoed them and pulled them to dry ground. "Riding bog" was just another chore the cowboys were saddled with. For ranch managers like

Goodnight, however, the heel flies were a serious problem, as the harassed cattle could not eat normally and ran off pounds, and that cost serious money at sale time.

Range fires were another hazard in the Panhandle, destroying thousands of acres of grass and killing livestock. They were worse in the fall and winter, when strong winds whipped across tinder-dry grass ignited by lightning, a carelessly attended campfire, or a cowboy's discarded cigarette. The fires were worst on the great uninterrupted sweeps of the Llano, but they also were a hazard in the Palo Duro. In the 1920s Goodnight recalled gratefully that he had had "very limited" experience fighting fires. He did, however, remember one year he had over a thousand miles of furrows plowed to reduce fire risk. Depending upon the terrain, two or three parallel rows were plowed, fifteen to twenty feet apart, and the intervening grass burned. That could restrict fire in the canyon because winds were seldom as high there as on the Llano, where the JA had summer pastures. Up there, desperate measures were resorted to, such as splitting cows and having two cowboys drag the bloody sides of the corpse along the downwind edge of the fire. These tactics cost cows, and sometimes the horse on the fire side had hooves permanently injured.

Some of the problems facing the Panhandle rancher were mentioned in a census supplementary report, "Enumeration of Live Stock on Farms in 1880." The sources cited for the Panhandle were Joseph G. McCoy, certainly an authority on the cattle industry; the commandant of Fort Elliott; and "Charles Goodnight, esq., Clarendon, Donley County," probably his mailing address. The census correctly located him in Armstrong County. The entire population of the Panhandle was computed at 1,607, again, in an area roughly the size of the state of West Virginia, and no inhabitants were located in six of the twenty-six counties.

The enumerator for the district including Armstrong County was C. H. Kimball, the JA's bookkeeper, so we may assume the accuracy of the count that totaled thirty-one for that county. Kimball listed the Goodnight household as including—besides

Charles Goodnight, left, addressing his bookkeeper (holding the door open). Courtesy Western History Collections, University of Oklahoma Libraries, Norman, Oklahoma.

Charles and Mary—himself, Goodnight's brother-in-law, Albert M. Dyer, and a cook. The Goodnights appear as "Stock Grower" and "Keeping House." A second household on the ranch consisted of a dairyman and his wife and their two young daughters.

Other people enumerated were another cook, a blacksmith, a laborer, sixteen "herders," and a foreman. That the census was taken in early June, a busy cattle-working period, accounts for the relatively large number of cowboys. If the census had been taken in the late fall or winter, the number of household members would have been significantly fewer. The man listed as foreman was John E. Farrington, whose judgment on cattle Goodnight trusted implicitly, although he doubted that Farrington, an unpolished character, could make the transition to a more-civilized society, a judgment others might have made about Goodnight himself.

In Randall County, adjoining Armstrong on the west, only three inhabitants were located. One of them, another Goodnight brother-in-law, Walter M. Dyer, was also listed as a stockman. After coming to the Panhandle with Goodnight, together with his brother Leigh and another youth, Walter had bought 320 acres near the site of Canyon, Texas, and launched a small cattle operation.

In 1877 Goodnight entrusted Leigh Dyer to conduct the first cattle drive from the Palo Duro to Dodge City. It was about 250 miles and ran essentially north-northeast, roughly the bearing of the North Star. On a landscape lacking conspicuous physical features, lining up the chuck wagon's tongue with the star to mark the end of the day's drive gave the drovers a heading when the group broke camp early the next morning. Like Charles Goodnight, other cowmen did not carry compasses.

In 1878 Goodnight himself led the drive, remarking years later that Dyer "really didn't make much of a trail." The boss also chose to travel away from the route followed by the freighters, whose livestock could be counted on to eat the grass along the trail down to the roots. Both Goodnight and Dyer averaged about twelve miles a day, and both simplified their task by keeping the herd moving behind Old Blue.

Old Blue was a Texas longhorn with a brass bell around his neck whose tinkle the cattle soon learned to follow. This is not strange bovine behavior to anyone who has seen cows traveling to the barn twice a day to be milked. They generally arrive behind the leadership of one cow and go to their assigned stations. Early in his driving days Goodnight had observed a similar phenomenon on the trail and simply built on that after recognizing Old Blue's tendency to dominate. The steer was only three years old when the drive to Dodge City began. With the bell around his neck, Old Blue would head up the trail on signal, and the other cattle would fall in behind. At the end of the day's drive a cowboy would tie the clapper in place, hobble the bell-steer, and the herd, hopefully, would graze and then settle down for the night. When they reached Dodge City, Old Blue learned to lead the cattle to the loading chute, step aside at the last minute, and watch the cowboys work the cattle up the chute and into the cars.

It did not always go so smoothly. The Mobeetie, Texas, newspaper once reported: "A herd of Mr. Goodnight stampeded one night recently on the trail to market, and were all scattered excepting two or three hundred. These were mostly the cattle that got into such a way of running on the trail last fall as to be unfit for market on their arrival at Dodge City, and were returned to the ranch." After that fiasco, Goodnight must have been difficult to be around for weeks.

On the return trips to the JA, Old Blue would keep pace with the cow ponies. Once back at the home ranch, he pretty much was free to munch grass and reflect on his special status. When needed to help control other cattle, he was available. A once-in-a-lifetime service occurred when he was drafted to help deliver back to the JA two young buffalo that Goodnight purchased from a ranch that had gone broke and was disposing of its assets. Old Blue, with one yoked to either side of him, brought them safely to their new home. When he finally died his horns were installed on the door to the vault in ranch headquarters.

Dodge City, the destination of most of the drives from the JA, also was the source of most of the supplies consumed on the ranch for its first decade, although in the earliest years they came from Trinidad, Colorado, about a four-hundred-mile haul. The freight was carried by wagons drawn by either oxen or mules. The latter were faster but had to be fed corn or oats, whereas the oxen grazed along the way. Hence there were two rates quoted, grass, or the more-expensive corn, as Goodnight well understood from his early days as a freighter. The wagons varied in size, but a large Studebaker could carry seven thousand pounds (greater than the capacity of the C47 transport plane operated by the Air Force in World War II). According to José Ynocencio, who worked as a teamster in his youth, a common arrangement was three wagons hitched in tandem and pulled by eight to twelve oxen or mules. They hauled to the JA everything the ranch required, from matches, canned goods, and boxed bacon to lumber and barbed wire. Freighters always needed a back load, and frequently in the early days this consisted of buffalo bones, worth about seventeen dollars a ton in Dodge City. Wagons returning from the JA might be carrying cedar posts, as the tree abounded in the canyons of the Palo Duro, especially Mulberry.

By the early 1880s, railroads began to build closer to the JA, and the Dodge City haul gave way to freighting from Texas locations, Colorado City, Wichita Falls, and in 1885, Harold, Texas. In 1887, when the railroad reached Clarendon, Texas, the JA began operating its own freight wagons to supply the ranch, requiring two days for the round-trip.

Under Charles Goodnight's obsessive control, guided by his powerful vision of what a Panhandle ranch should be, and subsidized by John George Adair's financial resources, the JA had made remarkable progress in just a few years. But the character of Panhandle ranching would be altered as word spread of the money to be made by buying Texas cattle cheaply and fattening them on free grass.

CHAPTER 6

The Panhandle Boom

THE Texas Panhandle enjoyed a period of rapid growth and a robust ranching boom in the first half of the 1880s, and Charles Goodnight and the JA were swept along with it. Competition for land and water intensified as word spread of the money to be made in cattle on the plains. Financiers, merchants, and industrialists seeking investment opportunities, as well as their counterparts in the British Isles, were excited by stories of quick profits to be made in ranching.

The formula for making money included free grass, cheap labor, and longhorn yearlings bought for about fifteen dollars a head and sold two years later for double that amount. The grass certainly was available, so long as the rancher could take advantage of a lax state government that would enable him to hold thousands of acres without paying a cent. Cowboys came cheap, at about twenty-five dollars a month plus keep. One enthusiast claimed that they, like the cattle, could survive the winters without shelter: "A cowboy scorns a tent, and will roll himself in a blanket and sleep under the open canopy of heaven, often during the entire round of seasons." One must wonder how much experience this "expert" had had with the howling northers that could sweep down the plains and make survival a challenge for beast and man. Another writer, this one for a Colorado livestock journal, believed that profits in the cattle industry were inevitable: "Cattle is one of those investments man cannot pay too much for, since if left alone, they will multiply, replenish and grow out of a bad bargain."

Still another misleading estimate came from someone who should have known better. James S. Brisbin, an active duty

Charles Goodnight, ca. 1880, at the peak of his career as a rancher. Courtesy Western History Collections, University of Oklahoma Libraries, Norman, Oklahoma.

cavalry officer who had served throughout the plains, published a book in 1881, *The Beef Bonanza, or How to Get Rich on the Plains*. In it he mentioned Goodnight only in his earlier capacity as a drover, ignoring his ranching experience in Colorado and the flourishing JA properties in the Panhandle. Brisbin argued that an investment of $200,000 in Texas cattle "would double itself in four years, and pay a semi-annual dividend of eight percent."

John W. Iliff, a pioneer Colorado rancher who bought thousands of longhorns driven north by Goodnight, attributed his rapidly increasing fortune to "the cost of both summering and wintering [being] simply the cost of herding, as no feeding or sheltering is required." Iliff died well before the horrors of the big die-off in the terrible winter of 1885–1886 destroyed that illusion, along with the fortunes of many cattlemen.

The English and Scots in the early 1880s invested millions of pounds sterling all over the globe, and nowhere more enthusiastically than on the Great Plains, although their Argentine and Uruguayan ranches would prove more profitable. James Brisbin's publisher had an outlet in the United Kingdom, and English periodicals carried enthusiastic articles on the financial possibilities of the American cattle trade. An author in the *Fortnightly Review* summed it up: locate an unoccupied range, drive a herd of cattle on it, and begin ranching. "There is no trouble about title, deeds, surveyors, and lawyers," he enthused. Skeptics could be referred to the 1880 report of a commission of parliament that concluded that 33 percent profit was possible in ranching in the American West, giving the government's imprimatur to the speculation. Thus it is not surprising that British investors poured millions into ranching, and seventeen of their American ranches were in Texas.

John George Adair recognized his good fortune in having Charles Goodnight as a partner and manager of their properties and was happy to renew their contract when it expired in 1882. The new one, for five years, listed assets as 93,629 acres valued at $150,000, and 27,870 cattle worth, at twenty dollars per head, $557,400. The ranch's 164 horses and mules were estimated at

$8,529. Other property, probably equipment and buildings, was listed at $2,052. If from that figure $205,272 was deducted, representing Adair's investment, earning 10 percent interest, it left an estate of $512,708.48 in which Goodnight had a one-third interest, a tidy sum.

Most of the original contract's terms were simply renewed, although Goodnight did get a handsome raise of $5,000, making his annual salary $7,500, a substantial sum for those days. Adair, a landlord not noted for his generosity with his employees or tenants, clearly placed a high value on Goodnight's stewardship.

In the summer of 1883 the London *Times* cited a General M'Clellan, who offered Charles Goodnight as an example of what could be accomplished in Texas. "The largest ranch in the state," according to the general, "is that of Mr. Charles Goodnight, at the head of Red River. He began buying land only four years ago, and now he controls 700,000 acres. To enclose his landed possessions, 250 miles of fencing are required. He has the finest, though not the largest herd in Texas." Within a week the *Times* had to correct the record with a letter from John George Adair, writing from Rathdaire, his estate in Ireland. "The three ranches which form this property," observed Adair, "and cattle, 60,00 head, upon them belong to me, with the exception of one third of one of them, which by arrangement has passed to the gentleman named, who is the efficient manager of the entire, and who was the discoverer of its wonderful capabilities." Adair concluded with the statement that Texas law permitted him, an Englishman, to own land in the state. With uncharacteristic graciousness — the JA's hands, and Goodnight himself, disliked him intensely, and he had worn out his welcome with his wife's family with just one visit to their Genesee Valley estate — Adair had clarified who was the dominant partner in the JA operation.

General M'Clellan's reference to 250 miles of fences was a recognition of a development in the Panhandle that revolutionized ranching there as elsewhere. Goodnight had built his first sixty miles on the northern perimeter of the ranch as a "drift fence." Its purpose was to prevent cattle from ranches to the north of the JA from drifting down onto the Adair-Goodnight range as they moved south with the winter storms.

Goodnight's neighbor to the west chose not to extend the fence and, years later, Goodnight remembered smugly that cattle from the north seeking to bypass the JA's drift fence ended up as a problem for the neighbor. A disadvantage of such fences was that cattle doing what was natural to them, drifting south propelled by a blue norther, could find their way blocked by a fence, jam up against it, and die in droves.

As elsewhere, Panhandle ranchers quickly recognized other valuable uses to which wire fence could be put. The open range system had made it impossible to separate pastures except by having cowboys ride the line separating them, and that was costly and not completely effective. Fenced separate pastures dedicated to horses, to cows and their calves, to steers being fattened for the market, and to bulls, made selective breeding possible. They also helped isolate round-up and branding activities that disturbed other cattle and interfered with their conversion of grass to beef.

With his usual attention to detail, Goodnight proceeded with the fencing of the properties under his management, buying as much as 60,000 pounds of wire at a time. It is interesting to speculate on the conversations about wire fences he might have had with a neighbor, Joseph Glidden of DeKalb, Illinois, on one of his rare visits to Texas. Glidden, who is generally credited with inventing the most practical method of making barbed wire, purchased 60,800 acres and fenced it completely before driving a cow on it, something a barbed-wire magnate could do.

Glidden's ranch lay to the north of the JA. Just to the southeast of the JA was another ranch, the Quitaque, sometimes referred to as the F Range, consisting of about 140,000 acres. On Adair's orders, Goodnight had purchased it for Cornelia Adair and fenced it in 1882. Within the Quitaque fence, however, every other section belonged to a railroad, although for the time being Adair-Goodnight stock would graze it. That

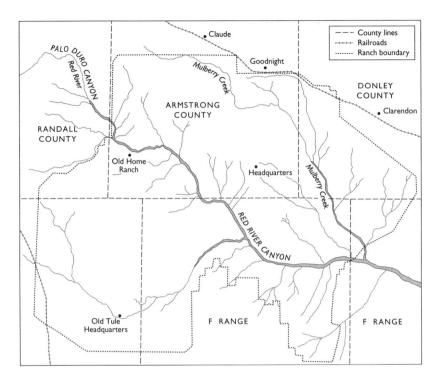

Panhandle ranches, based on a map by Doni J. Fox.

guaranteed trouble when the time came that settlers began to buy sections from the railroad.

After acquiring the Quitaque, Goodnight used more of the Adair-Goodnight partnership funds to purchase 170,000 acres that encompassed most of the Tule Canyon, which emptied into the Palo Duro from the south. Fencing for the Tule Ranch began the year it was bought, 1883, and completed the following year. Meanwhile, Goodnight put in a cross fence that divided the original ranch in the Palo Duro into two large pastures, henceforth referred to as JA and JJ. As the need arose, both were then subdivided to provide special-purpose pastures.

This construction of hundreds of miles of fence, much of it done by contractors after the fence, posts, gates, and other items needed had been purchased by the freight car–load, was a costly operation, usually over two hundred dollars a mile. Some of the first ranchers into the Panhandle had difficulty raising the funds required, and many of them took advantage of the ranching boom to sell out at a nice profit. And it made it even nicer if they sold, as was usually the case, to wealthy individuals or corporations with little experience and a willingness to take book count of the herds involved. The alternative was an expensive and time-consuming head count. The purchasers frequently paid good money for cattle that were nonexistent. When bondholders closed down one Panhandle cattle outfit, they found only 13,000 head of the 60,000 carried on the books.

The fenced pastures simplified Goodnight's plans to upgrade the Adair-Goodnight herds. And the rancher's views on what breed of bull to employ changed over time. He had begun with Durham sires, then experimented with Black Angus, before finally settling on the white-faced Herefords as the ideal beef producer. Most of the Herefords he purchased from a man who would become a longtime friend and ally in the political battles in the Panhandle, Oliver H. Nelson, known to most as Judge Nelson after two years presiding over a county court.

Goodnight regarded Nelson as the foremost authority on cattle in Texas. From him he had first purchased hundreds of Durhams, but by the mid-1880s, Nelson had become convinced that the Hereford was the superior animal, and Goodnight began acquiring that breed from him and never looked back. The Hereford had the stamina and hustle to survive in the Great Plains environment and, when mated with the longhorn-Durham cross, produced fine beef animals.

John Clay, reminiscing about his decades of experience with livestock and ranch management, waxed enthusiastic about Charles Goodnight's accomplishments as a cattle breeder. He remembered his own maneuvers to buy, at the best price, four thousand JA steers, "a magnificent bunch of cattle . . . my admiration of Goodnight as a cattleman soared." The Scot also commented on the "F [Quitaque] cattle, another of Charlie Goodnight's creations in the Panhandle. Wonderful steers they were."

Oliver H. Nelson, a rancher and cattle dealer, and Goodnight's best friend. Courtesy Western History Collections, University of Oklahoma Libraries, Norman, Oklahoma.

In addition to acquiring high-grade sires, Goodnight improved his stock by culling the less-desirable cows. Also, when there was a poor market for both calves and cows he spayed some of the lower-grade cows, initially using tools he personally had designed. This was an innovation that his fellow ranchers derided, arguing that natural increase was the greatest asset of the rancher. In time they changed their minds while Goodnight went on to employ veterinarians for this procedure and spay as many as seven thousand cows and heifers in a season.

Improving the breed was important, but Goodnight, like all Panhandle ranchers, had a water problem that limited the number of cattle that his pastures could carry, particularly those on the Llano. There, in the best of years, a few weeks without rain would see the smaller streams dry up and the grass stop growing. As the cattle, unlike those fed and sheltered throughout the winter in other regions, were supposed to survive in the open and feed off the grass that cured standing into nutritious hay, it was essential that the ranches get rain at proper intervals. If it did not rain, they had to sell off cattle — usually at a loss — as all ranchers in the area were being forced to sell, or rent pasture in better-watered areas elsewhere.

The Adair-Goodnight holdings were better off than those exclusively on the Llano. The Prairie Dog Fork of Red River flowed through the canyon and was fed by streams originating in the smaller canyons that emptied into the Palo Duro. When possible, however, Goodnight preferred to save the canyon pastures for winter grazing and at other times throw the cattle on the Llano that had no real streams, only the ephemeral playas.

To maximize their water supply the ranchers came to rely on a number of techniques, including scrapings, construction of stock tanks to hold runoff from springs and small streams, drilled wells, and windmills. *Scrapings* was a translation of a Spanish term, *los escarbadas,* which the Mexicans employed for the technique. They learned that even if the streambed was dry, usually they could dig a hole in it and water would gradually rise to the surface. Goodnight had learned in his cattle-driving days that simply allowing cattle to mill around in a dry water course could produce some water.

Water from springs that were prevalent in the Palo Duro and tributary canyons could be channeled to troughs for the cattle, or for home use, as when the Old Home Place was located so as to take advantage of a nearby spring. Also, streams could be dammed to produce "tanks" for watering livestock. These could be constructed by ranch hands, although for the larger tanks the job might be given to contractors who went from ranch to ranch with their equipment and crews. Tanks, however, did tend to silt up, and their dams could be eroded by cattle standing on them, so maintaining and replacing tanks became a significant expense in the eighties. That decade also saw the introduction of drilled wells and the windmills that could pump the water to the surface.

The first drilled well on the JA resulted from Goodnight's connections with Colonel B. B. Groom, manager of the Francklyn Land & Cattle Company, a large operation to the north of the JA. Colonel Groom had had experience raising cattle in Kentucky, but was largely ignorant of the techniques for a successful operation on the plains. He needed counseling badly, and Goodnight was one upon whom Groom depended, seeking the veteran's advice on everything from a proper brand design to the type of land to acquire. As Groom informed his superiors: "He was very cordial and asked me to come to see him; that it had cost him years and thousands of dollars to learn some very simple little things which he would present to me free."

In turn, Goodnight felt free to call upon Groom for favors. When the Kentuckian had the first well-drilling machine in the Panhandle, Goodnight asked him to drill a well in the Palo Duro, for which he would pay. Although Groom needed the crew and equipment for more drilling on the spread he managed, the Diamond F, he justified to his superiors his acquiescence to Goodnight's request. It seemed that Goodnight had been appointed as appraiser in a land dispute in which the Francklyn Land & Cattle Company was involved. "We could easily make the well back to us with a few cents per acre,"

Groom advised his superiors. "On the other hand he [Good-night] could make us pay more than the value. So I thought it best to have him certainly for us than likely against us in the matter." It is not likely that a man of Goodnight's probity would have sold out for the use of a well-drilling outfit, but clearly Groom was taking no chances.

Windmills made deep wells practical, as the force of the wind, of which there was plenty on the Great Plains, could be harnessed to draw the water to the surface and empty it into a tank. A simple device to inactivate the pump when the water reached a certain level eliminated overflowing. But there was a downside; the first windmills required a lot of maintenance and if a ranch had many — the large spreads would have dozens — one ranch hand would be assigned the chore. He would be constantly on the move from one tower to the next, lubricating and making minor adjustments and repairs, a lonely occupation.

Obviously no rancher could afford to spend over two hundred dollars a mile for fencing, and over two hundred dollars for a drilled well and windmill, for land to which he did not have clear title. Goodnight was well aware of this and was constantly pressing Adair for funds to acquire a clear title, or at least leases to as much of the land as they could possibly afford of the many hundreds of thousands of acres the partners had monopolized. Land problems resulting from pressure from the state to realize income from its public domain, and conflicts with settlers seeking homesteads, and with rustlers, were complicated by the absence of fundamental forms of government. Given the large holdings of the JA and the force of his personality, it was inevitable that Charles Goodnight would play a leading role in the establishment and maintenance of a more ordered society in the Panhandle.

CHAPTER 7

Toward a More Ordered Society

IN the nineteenth century many Americans migrated from one frontier area to another before finally settling down. Charles Goodnight's family had made several such moves, and as an adult he was noted for establishing new trails as a cattle drover. Giving up that occupation, he settled down as a rancher in the Pueblo, Colorado, area, where he played an important role in community and stock-raising affairs. Although rugged individualists by any definition, Goodnight and fellow ranchers recognized the necessity of cooperation in areas of mutual concern, such as range rights.

The evolution of the open-range system on the Great Plains was founded on the practice of honoring the claim of the first man to occupy with his stock a stretch of the banks of a stream. This gave him the right, by custom, to that water and the pastures on either side, going back as far as the cattle would graze, usually about seven to eight miles. In the absence of land titles and courts to enforce them, an acceptance of that simple principle by every cattleman was the condition that made the open range system workable.

Given the absence of fences — barbed wire did not reach the plains until about 1880, and the cost of rail fences on the treeless plains was prohibitive — inevitably there was some intermingling of cattle from neighboring ranches. This was especially a reality during the winter months, when they drifted south before the harsh northerly blasts. This migration made it necessary to hold spring roundups, requiring the cooperation of all the cattlemen of an area. For example, in the spring of 1880 the roundup began with the Adair-Goodnight stock and included all ranches in the Panhandle between the Red and Canadian rivers, a block of land one hundred miles wide. The principal mission of the roundup was to sort out the cattle and brand the new calf crop to ensure that every rancher's stock would carry his brand and any other identifying marks he employed. The best-known of the latter were those of Goodnight's old business associate, John Chisholm. His jingle bob cut of his cattle's ears, causing a portion of the ear to dangle, and his rail brand, a line burned on the animal's side from shoulder to rump, were recognized throughout the Southwest.

Another roundup in the fall was done ranch by ranch to cut out the steers to be sent to market, plus any cows and bulls culled from the herd. In normal times the rancher retained his best cows and bulls, at a ratio of about one bull to fifteen cows.

Rustlers were another factor forcing ranchers to cooperate. A single cattleman was virtually at the mercy of thieves if his neighbors turned a blind eye to the rustlers, to the illegal activities of their own cowhands and the nesters who had homesteaded within their pastures. Goodnight had helped launch a movement in southeast Colorado to cope with these and other problems. He and fellow ranchers, including Henry W. Cresswell, who later would follow Goodnight into the Panhandle and establish one of the most successful ranches in the area, the Bar CC, first met in the fall of 1868 to discuss their concerns. That led three years later to the organization of a stockmen's association that drafted rules for conducting roundups, registering brands, coping with scrub bulls on the open range, excluding sheepmen, and cooperating against rustlers. That organization, incidentally, preceded by about six years the formation in Graham, Texas, of the Northwest Texas Cattle Raisers Association by Goodnight's old friend C. C. "Lum" Slaughter and other prominent cattlemen. With that type of experience it is no surprise that Goodnight would attack similar problems in the Panhandle by urging united action.

Rustlers were an expensive burden in the Panhandle. Goodnight would later attribute their numbers to the Panhandle being "bounded on the north by the Indian Nation [Cherokee

Outlet], a cradle for outlaws, on the west by New Mexico, a virtually lawless country and on the south by Old Mexico." The professional criminals included the celebrated Billy the Kid, whose gang, operating from a base in New Mexico, rustled cattle in the Panhandle; and Dutch Henry, with whom Goodnight earlier had struck a deal. But most of the ranchers' losses were at the hands of enterprising cowboys. The story of the man who appeared in an area driving a lone steer, and within two years had accumulated a nice little herd — all the product of that steer — was a bitter joke about a serious problem.

The methods employed by the cowboys gone wrong evolved over the years. Their favorite targets were the mavericks, cattle old enough to have left the side of their mothers, but which had escaped branding. The rustler would cut these out of a herd carrying the rancher's brand and burn his own. Calves were even stolen from their mothers and held until they would begin to eat grass and give up trying to escape. A riskier procedure was to alter the brand on an animal, using a poker-shaped running iron to convert an *S* into an *8,* or an *F* to an *E,* to cite only the simplest of almost limitless alterations possible. As it soon became too risky to be caught with a running iron, thieves began to employ less-conspicuous tools, like a piece of baling wire or a portion of a horseshoe.

In 1879, in response to pleas from desperate ranchers, the state ordered into the Panhandle a ranger detachment commanded by Captain George Washington Arrington, better known as Cap, who had an unusual background for a lawman. Born John C. Orrick in Alabama, he had served the Confederate cause as a member of Mosby's guerrillas. After the war, when the South was occupied by the federal army, he had killed a black man and fled to Central America. Returning to the United States, he settled in Texas under his new name and, in 1875, enlisted in the Texas Rangers, rising to the rank of captain in only three years. In the Panhandle, Arrington made serious inroads on the criminal element and also confronted the colonel commanding Fort Elliott on the issue of jurisdiction over local Indians. Charles Goodnight's first contact with Arrington

came when Cap arrived alone and unannounced at the JA headquarters. The rancher sensed something was wrong and
quizzed Arrington, who admitted that he was a Ranger and had
a warrant for the ranch's blacksmith. That issue was quickly
resolved, and Goodnight and Cap became fast friends. Meanwhile the Ranger proved his mettle by making many arrests.

Arresting, however, was only the initial step in law enforcement. Appearance before a judge was the next procedure, but
in the Panhandle courts were hard to find; indeed, there was
not a single county government until 1879. Until then the nearest Texas court was at Henrietta, about two hundred miles from
the mouth of Palo Duro Canyon. Finally, in the spring of 1879
the first Panhandle county, Wheeler, was organized. Traders in
buffalo hides had established the settlement of Sweetwater,
subsequently named Mobeetie, and it was also the home of the
newly established Fort Elliott, whose garrison kept the merchants and saloon operators in business after the decline in the
hide trade. As Goodnight recalled it, Wheeler County mustered the required quota of legal voters by using, without their
permission, the names of cowboys completely unaware of the
move to organize a county government.

Goodnight also had been of the opinion that at the county
seat every official except the county judge, but including the
sheriff, was "living illicitly with a prostitute." He was willing
to concede, however, that the sheriff who had been a saloon
keeper and gambler, besides making an honest woman of his
consort, proved to be a competent lawman.

Judges from Gainesville and Sherman presided over the first
two state court sessions in Mobeetie, but in 1881 the state
organized a new judicial district centered in Wheeler County
and having jurisdiction throughout the Panhandle. The first
judge was Frank Willis, who would become a rather reluctant
ally of Charles Goodnight in the growing state land leasing
controversy. The rancher credited Judge Willis with improving
the moral climate of Wheeler County when, at his first court
session, "true bills were found against every officer except himself, Dubbs [the county judge] and Fleming [the sheriff],

which broke up the illicit living and was the beginning of actual enforcement of law." But Mobeetie was about seventy miles from JA headquarters, and Goodnight was pleased when Donley County, whose seat, Clarendon, was only about twenty miles away, was organized in 1882. Indeed, the rancher had played a major role in bringing about that development.

It was appropriate that Charles Goodnight, a vocal critic of drunkenness—although not averse to a drink with friends—should have as his closest neighboring community Clarendon, founded in 1878 as a temperance colony. Its early settlers, some twenty-five or thirty families, came from a number of eastern states under the leadership of a young Methodist minister, Lewis Henry Carhart. With the assistance of relatives, the Reverend Carhart managed to buy 343 sections of railroad land, and the first settlers located in Donley County, as yet unorganized. The first edition of the town's newspaper referred to the community as a "sobriety settlement." Soon cowboys, including those from the JA, which occupied much of the southwest corner of the county, were referring to the town as Saints Roost. Early on it did have seven Methodist ministers propagating the faith and competing for parishioners.

Goodnight was not impressed by his first contact with his new neighbors, finding them long on enthusiasm and short on practical experience, as evidenced by their pitching tents on flats prone to flood. But, as was his wont with newcomers generally, the rancher was generous with his advice on everything from building sod structures to exploiting local plant and game resources. And when the Saints platted a town and sold lots, he helped them maintain their purity by confronting a rough individual who had purchased some of the lots with the idea of opening a saloon, despite the vociferous objections of the Saints. Goodnight confronted the man and pointed out a grove of cottonwoods with an ample supply of limbs stout enough to support a noose. The entrepreneur abruptly concluded to take his merchandise elsewhere. A Goodnight biographer, Laura V. Hamner, emphasized that the rancher, as usual, was unarmed—she titled her work *The No-Gun Man of*

Texas — but his formidable size and stern demeanor intimidated this man as with so many others.

Clarendon would fit in well with Goodnight's plans to provide more protection for the area's stockmen. He would find allies in Thomas Bugbee, the man he had narrowly beat out for the title "First Rancher into the Panhandle"; Henry W. Cresswell, his old associate in efforts in the Pueblo area to unify the ranchers; and cattle dealer and rancher Oliver H. Nelson, who would become Goodnight's closest friend. A small, quiet man, fourteen years younger, Nelson had an inner strength that Goodnight respected, and he acknowledged that Nelson was an authority without peer on cattle. The four men began discussions that would lead to the creation of the Panhandle Stock Association, and it is no surprise that Goodnight took the lead in the organization process. He had had experience in Colorado with such an enterprise, but so had Cresswell. What Goodnight had as well was the unrivaled respect of his peers and the dynamism to keep such a process moving. His name was on the notice that announced a meeting of all interested parties to take place in Mobeetie early in 1880 to discuss the ranchers' common problems.

Actually two meetings in Mobeetie in 1880 were necessary to arrive at an organization plan, and not until the following year was the Panhandle Stock Association established, with John F. Evans, whose Spade Ranch was in Donley County, as its first president. He also served on the critical Protective and Detective Committee, as did Goodnight and two others. Membership was open to cattlemen at least nineteen years of age. Early in the Association's history Goodnight stopped cold a move to grant voting rights in proportion to the number of cattle owned. He told the membership that the intention had been "to give the little man equal rights with the big man and before I'd see such a rule passed, I'd disband the whole organization." But a democracy the Association was not, and it would be run by the big ranchers. Moreover, it should be noted that its membership included only about one-quarter of the ranchers in the

Panhandle, and that minority was found primarily in the eastern half.

The two high-priority problems that had led to the organization of the Panhandle Stock Association were rustlers and Texas fever. Cap Arrington and his Rangers had scared off some of the rustlers, but the surge of cattle into the area in the late seventies and early eighties encouraged a corresponding increase in the rustler population. The Association's response was similar to that of the Northwest Texas Cattle Raisers Association, led by men Goodnight knew well. A son of his old mentor, Oliver Loving, was active in the group, as were C. C. Slaughter and Kit Carter, both of whom Goodnight had been associated with in the aborted expedition to Mexico in 1866. The two organizations confronted similar problems and came up with similar solutions. It would seem logical that Goodnight and his associates were well aware of what went on east of them and possibly profited by their experience. Certainly both groups decided to assess members relative to the size of their herds and to hire inspectors to search for stolen stock.

The Panhandle Stock Association inspectors were located at Kansas City, St. Louis, Dodge City, Caldwell, and elsewhere. At St. Louis, for example, an inspector found that one steer in four in a sixteen-car shipment bore a brand not that of the shipper. Those steers were segregated, sold, and the income distributed among the legal owners of the stock. In August 1882 the *Dodge City Times* carried a story presumably describing that coup by the inspectors, and referred to another thirty-six head "being stopped after it was learned that the inspectors had them headed off both at Kansas City and St. Louis." The Association also had spies among the employees of suspected ranchers. For a fee, these undercover agents reported on anything of a suspicious nature. One target was a foreman who had been stealing from his gullible employer, who required some persuasion to be convinced of the man's guilt.

At the height of the crackdown by the Association, the rumor spread that its executive committee, which included

Goodnight, was organizing a vigilante commission. Years later Goodnight would recall, with satisfaction, that thirteen of its potential targets hurriedly left the area, delighting the Association members because it was quite difficult to get court convictions. Juries were packed with cowboys who had friends who had done a little mavericking, or had done it themselves. Frank Willis, the first judge of the newly created 31st Texas Judicial District, who held court alternately in Mobeetie and Clarendon, expressed his frustration at this phenomenon. Goodnight could only assure him that "if you will give me a jury" he would provide indictments. Judge Willis came to recognize, however, that convictions on rustling charges in his court would be few and far between. And Goodnight identified one problem: "The thieves can outswear you — they can swear to what is necessary, and you can't prove anything except the truth."

The Association even dispatched one of its men, John W. Poe, to New Mexico to assist authorities there to run down Billy the Kid, who had been making inroads on herds in the western Panhandle. As late as the 1920s Goodnight was still lauding Poe, a former sheriff of Wheeler County, for backing up Sheriff Pat Garrett the night he killed the Kid. The Association did reduce significantly the incidence of rustling, and the widespread fencing of the mid-eighties greatly helped to discourage rustling by preventing the cattle from wandering, thus simplifying keeping them under observation. As rustling declined, the Association could focus on that other issue, the strange malady killing thousands of cattle.

Texas fever was a menace for farmers and ranchers throughout the Middle West and the Southern Plains when Texas longhorns, themselves immune to the disease, were driven north from their habitat in the southern part of the state. At the time there was no agreement on what the disease was or how it spread, although many speculated that longhorn fecal matter or saliva were possible transmitters. It was apparent that climate was a possible factor as cattle driven as far north as Wyoming no longer were a problem. Also, apparently time was a consideration because cattle carried out of Texas by railcar, moving at twenty miles per hour, were much more likely to carry the disease than herds walking thirteen or fourteen miles per day.

If there was doubt about its cause, there was none about its terrible impact. Walter Dyer, Goodnight's brother-in-law, had moved three hundred quality steers to a new range. His timing was disastrous. A short time later their pasture was crossed by a herd of longhorns being driven north. Within three weeks all of Dyer's herd were dead. His brother Sam, who was in business with their sister, Molly Goodnight, lost all but twenty-five of a herd of a thousand, a crushing blow. Oliver Nelson reported that the stock trading firm with which he was associated lost cattle worth $250,000 to the disease, from 1882 to 1884.

When he was in the business of driving cattle from Texas to northern markets, Charles Goodnight had been on the other side of this issue. One of his longtime employees, John Rumans, remembered a confrontation between his boss and armed Coloradans determined to block the transit of a Goodnight herd. A lengthy parley ensued, finally terminated by an exasperated Goodnight, who ordered his men forward. While they unsheathed their Winchesters he brandished a shotgun and bellowed: "I've monkeyed as long as I want with you sons of bitches!" As the herd surged ahead the cowed Coloradans drew back and allowed it to pass. But by 1880 Goodnight was attempting to prevent other Texans from crossing his land and contaminating his cattle.

In August 1880 a fellow Texan, whom he knew well from his Palo Pinto County days, had a herd approaching the boundaries of the JA properties. Goodnight sent him a note advising him to take another route north, concluding with the ominous words, "You will never pass through here in good health." But Goodnight had met his match. George T. Reynolds was a tough hombre, carrying an arrowhead in his body for sixteen years before having it surgically removed. He had been a Pony Express rider and a Confederate cavalryman, and had driven cattle from Texas to New Mexico before Goodnight and Loving ventured into the business. Reynolds was furious at Goodnight's ultimatum and had it published in the *Fort Griffin Echo,* in order that "stock men may know generally how overbearing prosperity can make a man." More to the point, his herd crossed JA land, and Goodnight did not challenge him. This was one episode that he did not reminisce about in his old age.

Through the Panhandle Stock Association, Goodnight and his fellow members could speak with more authority, imposing the celebrated Winchester Quarantine. They basically proclaimed all the Panhandle off limits for cattle from south Texas, while offering an alternative trail that approximately followed the Panhandle's eastern and northern boundaries. To make it more acceptable, member ranchers constructed tanks to provide water for the herds on the trail. For those not susceptible to persuasion, well-armed riders, paid over twice the prevailing wages for cowboys, patrolled a line just south of Cornelia Adair's Quitaque Ranch. They would hold potential intruders in place until cooperative Panhandle judges could issue injunctions barring their farther progress.

One trail boss who was reluctant to take the longer route that minimized risk to Panhandle herds was confronted by Goodnight and Oliver Nelson in person. Those two riders were being followed, at some distance, by a wagon carrying several well-armed men. Goodnight warned the trail boss that they had a "wagon full of Sharp-shooters and an injunction coming from Mobeetie as fast as horse can bring it. Which do you want?" He chose to go around, and the crisis ended. The Winchester Quarantine reduced markedly the loss of Panhandle cattle to Texas fever.

Not until after the turn of the century would it be conclusively demonstrated that ticks dropping from Texas longhorns had been the source of the problem. That the ticks were sensitive to low temperatures explained why cattle driven into the Central and Northern Plains ceased to be carriers. With ticks identified as the culprits, cattle dips were developed to rid the animals of the pests. Meanwhile, Goodnight, with his lively curiosity about anything related to nature, observed that suckling calves did not contact the fever even if their mothers were contagious. For those interested in introducing purebred stock into contaminated areas, he advised that they do it by sending calves that would suckle local cows and thereby achieve immunity. Nevertheless, the fundamental problem remained, and remains. Today about sixty "tick riders," Department of Agriculture employees on horseback, patrol the Rio Grande boundary. Their job is to intercept stray cattle and horses from Mexico and dip them in pesticide. But the fear now, however, is that tick variants resistant to pesticides may be developing south of the border.

But Charles Goodnight and his fellow ranchers contributed more than Winchester Quarantines and antirustler campaigns toward a more ordered Panhandle society. They had both the numbers and financial resources to make a difference. For example, local and county governments had difficulty recruiting and retaining public servants because the salaries and fees associated with their positions were miserably inadequate. The Panhandle Stock Association levied its members to subsidize salaries of officials of both Wheeler and Donley counties. This amounted to $2,500 annually for the Donley County attorney, $1,500 for the sheriff, and $1,000 for the judge, and the needs of public education also were recognized.

One day Goodnight was in Clarendon, and the county judge called his attention to the fact that the town had no school. Although neither Goodnight nor any of the other ranchers had children who would attend, he promptly broached the subject with the Association's executive board, and it raised enough money to operate a school. He also helped recruit a teacher, a young ranch hand best known for his exuberant lifestyle. Goodnight gave him a qualified endorsement: "We ought to hang him, but I guess it is better to put him to work." And Oliver Nelson offered an interesting explanation for the Association's charity: "We had no school tax and did not want any," which makes their action appear somewhat less noble. As it was, they had to carry the burden only two years until Donley County was able to organize a school district and tap into funds from the sale of state school lands.

Goodnight contributed his time and energy to other civic

responsibilities. He served as a county commissioner and an election commissioner. He put in time in the jury box and also headed grand juries. One of these for Wheeler County, with Goodnight chairing, rendered a report in December 1881 that provided some insights on county jail conditions in the winter and the problem of streetwalkers. "The floors of the jail," the jurors observed, "are of iron and prisoners are not provided with mattresses or anything to shield them from contracting rheumatism or other diseases."

Their report also complained that the character of Mobeetie, which had begun as an adjunct to Fort Elliott and its garrison, was changing for the better. "Many respectable families reside here at the present time," the report read. Therefore, "while we have no desire to prosecute or oppress women of this character in their unfortunate and fallen condition yet we think that the plying of their vocation and wanton behavior on the public streets and in broad daylight is something which a common sense of decency alone calls for suppression." But members of the jury headed by Goodnight made clear that they were only opposed to the public display on the streets: "Women of this character live and ply their vocation elsewhere and we see no reason why the same cannot be controlled in this place." In later life Goodnight would declare, "I have only known good women and I never wanted to know anything about the bad ones, and I don't feel that a man has any right to talk about them, even if they are bad."

One of the good women he had known was Lulu Miller Frye. Later she related an episode involving Goodnight that illustrates how primitive the Panhandle had been in the late 1870s. The Fryes were living in a two-room cabin a few miles from Fort Elliott while trying to get a start in ranching. One night, when her husband was away trying to locate some missing cattle, she heard a man hailing the house. Initially she kept quiet, fearful it might be some drunken soldier from the post. But she did respond when addressed by name, and the individual identified himself as Charles Goodnight, who, together with a companion, was desperate for food and somewhere to spend the night. As she remembered it, "I was glad to see them and cooked their supper although it was midnight." Following that she directed them to the other room in the house that contained a bed made of split poles, covered with gunny sacks filled with prairie hay. The next morning she provided breakfast, and the men departed after declaring "that it was the best bed and breakfast they had ever enjoyed. They went on their way and I felt almost lonely enough to cry."

It was a raw country, and the few people there were dependent upon each other. Circumstances forced them to cooperate to survive. In the late seventies and early eighties, Charles Goodnight and his fellow ranchers had addressed a variety of political and social problems and furthered the Panhandle's progress toward a more ordered society. But they began to face a serious economic threat to their access to free, or at least cheap, grass, the very foundation of their ranching enterprises.

CHAPTER 8

The Cattle Baron and
the Children's Grass

FROM 1880 to 1887 Charles Goodnight played the leading role in the ranchers' fight to maintain access to the millions of acres of state school land that lay in alternate sections throughout most of the Panhandle. Indeed, one of the first steps taken by the new Panhandle Stock Association was to send a lobbyist to Austin to seek passage of legislation enabling them to lease, at bargain rates, school lands that they had been monopolizing.

In the early eighties the ranchers had begun to fence in their customary ranges. This complicated life for the settlers, or nesters, as the big cattlemen commonly referred to them, hoping to homestead within the huge pastures preempted by ranchers like Goodnight. Even the *Dodge City Times,* with a vested interest in the cattle trade, would comment about sixteen railcar loads of barbed wire ordered by Goodnight and others: "The cattle business is becoming a monopoly in the Panhandle of Texas."

The ranchers also found little sympathy in Austin, where the legislature was dominated by members whose constituents were predominantly East Texas farmers and the businessmen they patronized. People of that stripe looked upon the state's public lands as "the children's grass," a source of funds for public education. As early as 1879 the legislature had authorized the sale of the Panhandle school land, although there were as yet only a small handful of settlers there. When the cattlemen did buy they selected not large blocks of thousands of acres, but rather a few scattered sections to solidify their hold on the available surface water. Goodnight had the good fortune to have a partner who had made a career of buying land on mortgage, and he could be persuaded that they should expedite their purchases to solidify their hold on the Palo Duro. But even there large sections remained in the public domain, although fenced in by Goodnight.

The state legislature, however, was in the hands of people who believed that Texas's future lay with the homesteader, the same principle that underlay the federal government's land system, which had determined that 160 acres was the proper foundation for rural life. The Texas law enacted in 1879 provided for a limit to sales, at fifty cents an acre, to blocks no larger than 640 acres, at least a recognition that in the Panhandle conditions required larger tracts for settlers to survive.

The Texas land commissioner from 1878 to 1887 was William C. Walsh, who had taken office to find, to his dismay, that the commission had shown little interest in protecting the state's patrimony from assorted crooks. He promptly brought suit against land thieves, sending thirty to the state penitentiary, and frightening dozens of others into fleeing Texas. He was not happy with the 1879 law because it called for only half of the income from land sales to go into the public school fund, the other half to be applied to the state debt. Walsh did support the legislation enacted in April 1883 providing for the competitive leasing of school land at a minimum price of four cents an acre.

Charles Goodnight and his fellow ranchers also were happy with the new law. It made possible buying seven sections (4,480 acres) of unwatered state land at two dollars per acre or, if watered, at three dollars. This presumably was for the benefit of actual settlers, but Goodnight arranged to have their employees file on "a few of the important sections," which in time could be bought out by Adair and Goodnight. The ranchers also liked the leasing provision in the law, in large part because they all continued to recognize the land claims of their fellow ranchers and declined to try to outbid them. The Land Commission's response to this collusion was to arbitrarily raise the minimum fee to eight cents an acre. Its authority to do this was highly suspect, and the ranchers waged a campaign to force it to accept their four-cent bids. Charles Goodnight was the most conspicuous rancher activist in their fight to preserve their access to cheap grass.

The ploy the ranchers resorted to was to submit minimal bids, knowing there would be no competition. The Commission quickly caught on and refused to accept them. Then the ranchers' strategy was to get the Commission to just acknowledge their bids. Goodnight and William B. Munson, owner of the T Anchor Ranch that he had purchased from Leigh Dyer, joined together for the most dramatic of the efforts to register tenders with the Land Commission. Rejected initially, they walked to a nearby bank and negotiated a loan of nearly $100,000. Piling their cash in a wheelbarrow, they then hired a bank porter to trundle it up to the Land Commission. To discourage anyone seeking a shortcut to fortune, the ranchers strapped on six-shooters. They were accompanied by a prominent Austin lawyer, and former attorney general, W. M. (Buck) Walton. The rugged trio intimidated the official at the Land Commission into giving them a receipt for their tenders, all that they had hoped to get. With that safely in their hands, they returned the cash to the bank, paid $175 for the loan, and celebrated their triumph.

The struggle went on for over three years. A half-century later Goodnight and Oliver Nelson each provided their versions of events. The inevitable vagaries of memory influenced their personal reminiscences; however, they agreed on the broad picture. What is clear is that it was a crucial battle for the big ranchers and that one of the principal skirmishes was fought by a colorful cast of characters in the Donley County courthouse. Featured players besides Goodnight included Attorney General John D. Templeton, who had launched an effort to convict ranchers, specifically Goodnight, of fencing public land and failing to pay the proper rent.

In January 1886 the cases were tried in the court of Judge Frank Willis. Prosecuting was District Attorney W. H. Woodson, a rather mysterious figure who revealed little about his background, except that he was "an Englishman by birth, a Virginian by education, and a Texan by the grace of God." He bragged of not having a law library, but Woodson had a striking appearance and an effective courtroom presence. Tall, well dressed, with long black hair, he could quote scripture and shed tears with the best of them.

The grand jury addressed was one impaneled the previous July, and by coincidence had Goodnight himself as foreman; the other jurors were almost exclusively ranchers and their cowboys. Nevertheless, they followed protocol and found seventy-six true bills against ranchers, including their foreman and other jury members who were held to be occupying illegally some 3.5 million acres. The trial was held in Clarendon, only some twenty miles from the eastern perimeter fence of the JA Ranch. Given the paucity of population from which to draw jurors, it was inevitable that some of those chosen were JA employees. Nevertheless, Goodnight felt it imperative to have the best legal defense Adair money could buy. Of his three attorneys, the best known in the Panhandle was James N. Browning, a member of the Texas legislature who was more closely associated with the small stockmen who opposed big ranchers like Goodnight. Nevertheless, Browning could be hired and his reputation as "Honest Jim" could only contribute to Goodnight's defense. The rancher, however, would be outraged that Browning charged him twice the legal fees of his better-qualified attorney who had to travel all the way from Sherman, Texas, by way of Dodge City, to defend Goodnight.

The decision of Attorney General Templeton, who also served on the Land Commission, to not only direct District Attorney Woodson to press charges against the ranchers, but also to take the arduous trip to Clarendon himself, was indicative of his desire for a vigorous prosecution. He, however, had a supplementary agenda, to push the candidacy of Jim Browning for the judgeship held by Willis. Altogether, it was a most unusual judicial proceeding. Templeton and Goodnight, as the latter remembered it, had a confrontation seated on a log outside the courthouse. As the rancher remembered it, Templeton offered, if Goodnight would back Browning for the judgeship, to drop the charges against Goodnight. A man of honor, the rancher flatly refused to sell out his fellow defendants and made his refusal crystal clear: "I'd see you in hell first, farther than a wedge would fall in twenty years!"

Therefore the trial proceeded with the ranchers acknowledging that they had fenced in state school land, and the state agreeing that they had submitted legal bids of four cents per acre. Judge Willis then infuriated the attorney general by directing the jury to render not-guilty verdicts if they accepted as true the claims of the ranchers that they had tendered legal bids and the state acknowledged them. Templeton greeted the judge's action with an angry outburst, "I'll have you impeached for this!" It would be two hectic years for Charles Goodnight before the issue was finally resolved and new land legislation was enacted.

Goodnight and his allies won the first round when they backed Judge Willis in a successful bid for a second term. The general election brought many changes in the state hierarchy, a new governor and a new attorney general among them. The latter, Jim Hogg, continued Templeton's war on the ranchers. Judge Willis at first thought the time ripe to request the legislature to absolve him of the charges that they still had not addressed. But then he discovered that the Panhandle's representative, Jim Browning, and Senator Temple Houston, the latter the son of the legendary Sam, were not prepared to support him. Panicked, he drafted a letter of resignation, but Goodnight managed to intervene and persuade him to reconsider. To a reporter, the rancher denounced the Land Commission for depriving the state of nearly a half million dollars by refusing to accept the four-cent bids, and another three million because it had badly botched the sale of Panhandle land.

Then the fight moved to the legislature, where a House committee had been appointed to consider impeachment charges against Judge Willis, realizing his worst fears. But he would not fight alone. Charles Goodnight again retained Buck Walton and dispatched him to defend the timorous judge. Oliver Nelson, Cap Arrington, Goodnight, and other Panhandle ranchers and lawmen testified on behalf of Willis. Attorney General

Hogg took over the prosecution of Willis and produced witnesses from the anti–big rancher faction in the Panhandle. The *Galveston News* carried a story that could have been no comfort to the judge, or Goodnight either. It predicted impeachment and removal for Willis and referred to the "bullionaire" who should not act "in a lordly way," and denounced "the policy of allowing a few men to organize a county [Donley] and run it to suit their own convenience." Such sentiment was reflected in the House, and it voted to impeach.

That threw the contest into the Senate, where the House charges were debated. Some related to the Panhandle Stock Association's having subsidized the annual salaries of, among others, the Donley County sheriff and the district attorney to the tune of $1,000 and $1,500 respectively. This had been done openly in an effort to recruit capable individuals for poor-paying positions, but the anti-Willis forces put the worst possible face on it—"willful corruption." Nevertheless, Judge Willis made a personal statement to the senators that persuaded some, and the senators finally voted twenty-two to five to acquit. It was a victory not only for Willis but for Goodnight as well. The rancher, however, was in the midst of another battle over land legislation.

It was particularly aggravating to Goodnight that the Panhandle's only senator, Temple Houston, was leading the charge for the free-grassers, those trying to turn the clock back to when the Panhandle was open-range country and even a man with a hundred head of cattle could find a niche. To achieve this, Houston proposed to make fencing school lands a penal offense. Enforcement of such legislation would devastate the big ranchers who had spent thousands to fence state land and were willing to lease it at a reasonable figure.

Senator Houston was a flamboyant figure in his black frock coat and shoulder-length auburn hair topped off with a white Stetson. He liked to lace his arguments with literary allusions and could enthrall a courtroom or legislative chamber. Understandably, Goodnight feared that Houston could get his bill through, which would be a disaster for the JA and other large ranching operations. He again retained Buck Walton to assist him in his lobbying effort, yet they were clearly on the defensive. To Goodnight's frantic pleas for some successful stratagem, Walton finally proposed that he approach a man unknown to the rancher, and one who would be expensive — five thousand dollars, Walton estimated. Goodnight was desperate and promptly made contact with this miracle man, one George W. Clark, a Waco attorney and former state judge who was well connected in the legislature. In forty-eight hours Clark reported completion of mission to the amazed Goodnight, who declared, "I've been here two weeks and didn't do a thing!" The lobbyist's explanation was that he had misled some East Texas representatives about the identity of those behind the bill, although he may have dropped on them some of his five-thousand-dollar retainer to help them reach this conclusion.

There still remained the possibility of further land legislation, and Goodnight was forced to spend additional time in Austin. And lobbying continued to be expensive. Toward the end of the legislative session in the spring of 1887, he assured Cornelia Adair's agent, to whom he reported, that "our lease bill will pass. I have paid for it and should know." Goodnight estimated the total cost of that lobbying and the defense of Judge Willis at twenty thousand dollars. But it had been money well spent; the law passed in April provided for five-year leases at four cents per acre. With that assurance the big Panhandle ranchers could invest in the necessary fencing, drilling of wells and construction of tanks.

Some in the Panhandle were outraged, such as the editor of the *Tascosa Pioneer,* who bitterly opposed the big ranchers whom he accused of putting obstacles in the path of settlers and the development of the region. He collectively referred to them as "bullionaires," and when he heard that someone was considering doing a biography of Goodnight he reacted heatedly. "It is presumed," he observed bitterly, "the frontispiece will show a distinguished looking baron in the middle of a barbed wire empire." Little wonder that as late as 1889, the editor reported a rumor that Goodnight was retiring from ranching with a fervent: "If . . . the greatest of all cattle kings, has indeed sold out . . . the greatest living obstacle to the settlement of the Panhandle has been removed."

Being the target of so much hostility could wear on even someone as normally immune to criticism as Charles Goodnight. The verbal abuse he could endure up to a point, but legal harassment was harder to cope with. For example, in 1886 he was arrested for building a fence across a mail route that ran through a JA pasture. Goodnight maintained that he had simply moved a gate to detour a portion of the road that had washed out. Nevertheless, if the local federal commissioner ruled against him the rancher would have to travel two hundred miles to Guthrie, the site of the nearest federal court, to be tried.

Before his hearing in Mobeetie, he dropped by the commissioner's carpenter shop (being a federal commissioner was a part time job) and admired a bookcase the official was building. Learning that one like it would cost twenty-five dollars, Goodnight placed an order and left a check. When his case came up that afternoon the commissioner dismissed it, and Goodnight forgot about the bookcase. He clearly thought that he had bribed his way out of a considerable inconvenience. As he confided to Mrs. Adair, "I have again beaten them, nevertheless the business is getting monstrous and expensive. And I am disgusted with the whole ranch business."

The constant pressure on him to spearhead the lobbying in Austin, while managing the second-largest ranching empire in the Panhandle, had become too great a burden for him to endure. He definitely had health problems and at one time was reported to have succumbed to them while in Kansas. That led one of his critics to vigorously denounce him — until he remembered that as yet it was just a rumor. With visions of an outraged Goodnight descending upon him, he hastily backtracked: "But understand . . . if Uncle Charlie isn't dead, this talk don't go."

Goodnight's patience, never his strong suit, was exhausted by his need to report bimonthly the status of the ranches to

Mrs. Adair's agent in Italy, for whom he had a distinct dislike. For one who had always kept his own counsel and made decisions based on a lifelong experience in the cattle business, to have to seek approval of the Florence banker, William Henry Plunkett Maquay, was a constant irritant. It did not help that Maquay, who had had no ranching experience, was a purportedly illegitimate son of a man he had detested, John George Adair (who had since died). A further annoyance was that Maquay, as did Mrs. Adair, insisted on communicating by coded telegrams, for reasons of both security and economy. Goodnight preferred conventional letters such as he dictated to clerks in the JA Ranch headquarters. At one time he asked Mrs. Adair not to use the cable codes: "We can not interpret them here. . . . Operators muddle those ciphers up deliberately in order to force us to cable the other way." Whether or not this was the case, it was just another thing for him to worry about, and he was clearly weighed down by his multiple responsibilities and ill health. Goodnight concluded that he could no longer carry the burden.

January 20, 1886, Goodnight wrote Mrs. Adair, with a similar letter to Maquay. To her he announced: "I have been thinking the matter over for some time and I am satisfied both our interests would be best served by having a division and settling up in the summer of 1887. I now give you notice of dissolution during that year. I am having maps made up by the surveyor showing three equal divisions of the Ranch." For Maquay he added that rain was particularly short on Quitaque, and "it is the most desolate looking country you ever saw. . . . No one but an idiot would buy the Ranch in its present condition." Charles Goodnight's next two-and-a-half years can only be described as an ordeal as he dealt with Mrs. Adair, who did not want to give up her Texas properties, and with Maquay, whom Goodnight did not trust and believed was motivated only by his desire to inherit from John George Adair's estate the $100,000 he had been willed.

CHAPTER 9

The End of the
Goodnight-Adair Partnership

ALTHOUGH the widely publicized grass-lease fight had been
played out in the public arena, in the same time period Goodnight was having to carry the burden of the partnership with
Cornelia Adair. And this was at a time when ranching conditions in the Panhandle were at their worst since Goodnight had
arrived on the scene. Late in 1886, the year of the Big Die-up,
remembered for its severe drought and bitter cold, he estimated
that in the previous two years, one-third of the Panhandle cattle
perished, and in spring 1886 many horses died of the "itch."
Cattle prices continued to remain low and in 1887 Goodnight
was forced to pare the employment rolls until he was raising
cattle with the lowest ratio of men-to-cattle in the history of the
JA. In addition, he had to cut back on fence construction, halt-
ing work on a main line due to lack of funds.

One employee, James (Jack) Ritchie, did not suffer from the
cutbacks. He was the surviving son of two from Mrs. Adair's
first marriage. Jack had received his schooling, and his nickname Jacques, in France. After completing his education he had
associated with young men who his mother feared were leading
him astray. To provide a more wholesome atmosphere, early in
1886 she dispatched him to the JA to learn ranching under the
eagle eye of Charles Goodnight. The rancher took his super-
visory role seriously and kept the mother apprised of Jack's
performance. From the tone of his reports, Goodnight seems
to have become a champion of the young man, then in his mid-
twenties.

After several months as a cowboy, probably at wages of
about thirty dollars a month, Jack was raised by Goodnight to

fifty dollars, "not that he can possibly earn it," his supervisor informed Mrs. Adair. The idea was "to make him feel better and to make him think that he was of some importance, as you suggested." Goodnight also took him on a tour of all of the properties, providing a running commentary on all the aspects of stock raising that they observed, a marvelous opportunity for Jack to learn first-hand from an acknowledged expert on ranching in all of its manifestations. Goodnight hoped his training would be sufficient to "enable him to eventually run the business." The following March 1887, Goodnight reported to his mother that Jack "has acquired a good understanding of the business. . . . I think with a little advice [something Goodnight was never reluctant to give] he might make [*sic*] one of your ranches quite well."

As the months passed, Mrs. Adair began to suggest that her son return home. Goodnight's reaction was to observe that Jack, himself, was not interested in leaving, and, "I really think better stay on as he would only come in contact with old associates from which he will gain little." The rancher knew how to get to the mother.

Early in December, Goodnight again briefed Mrs. Adair on her son's performance, with which he declared himself to be "very well satisfied" and "think the more you trust him and the more responsibilities you can give him the better." He described Jack in terms that would make any mother's heart swell with pride: "energetic," "perfectly honest," "sober, and has shown no disposition to gamble here." The last apparently was one of his weaknesses. For the moment, Goodnight was so upbeat about him that he was planning to make Jack foreman of Tule Ranch, January 1, 1888, at a salary of one hundred dollars per month. A few days before doing so he apprised Mrs. Adair of his intention and remarked: "While he may not be as thoroughly competent as some hundred dollar men he is thoroughly in your interest and in my judgment the more you can crowd on him the better for you both." But Goodnight could not refrain from adding: "True he has much to learn about men and cattle, especially the latter."

To Goodnight's painful embarrassment, within a week of placing Jack in charge of Tule, he had to demote him. He had learned that Jack had gambled, a practice Goodnight viewed with abhorrence. To make matters worse, he had gambled with ranch employees, a potentially disruptive practice. Those with whom Jack had gambled were dismissed, and he demoted Jack, replacing him with L. C. Beverly. Goodnight's general communiqué to Tule personnel banning all drinking and gambling, concluded: "If Beverly does not obey this order I will send a man there who will." He then had the very sensitive task of informing Jack's mother. He tried to soften the blow by telling her that he, just before demoting her son, had had to fire Walter Dyer, his Quitaque manager and brother-in-law, for getting drunk in Clarendon and gambling. As yet he had not shared that news with Mary, and was not looking forward to it, "but business and my duty . . . demand it and I will do it if it costs my life." That was a bit dramatic, but Goodnight had deeply held principles. It is not surprising that at the close of his letter he declared, "I am heartily sick of men and ranches."

Mrs. Adair did soon recall her son from the ranch. Both she and Goodnight, however, must have been proud of Jack's subsequent record in the Boer War. Despite being an American citizen, he obtained a commission in the British cavalry and rose to the rank of major. Certainly he had been schooled by an outstanding leader of men.

On another less personal subject Goodnight and Mrs. Adair had disagreed earlier. He had employed a minor American artist, J. C. Cowles, a student and friend of the celebrated Albert Bierstadt, to paint ranch scenes, especially the geological wonders of Palo Duro Canyon, which over time would attract such well-known artists as Georgia O'Keeffe. Goodnight also had contracted with a photographer to provide prints of buildings and activities on the ranch. His motivations were purely mercenary; he hoped to use the prints and pictures to attract potential purchasers. But the Cowles connection with Albert Bierstadt had only produced additional tension in the Goodnight-Adair relationship. He had been led to believe that the celebrated painter, also a financial entrepreneur, might be interested in acquiring the JA properties, or in some way brokering their sale. However, when early in 1887 Goodnight tried to arrange a meeting between Mrs. Adair and Bierstadt in New York, she made clear that she resented his unauthorized initiative. He could only respond that he had gotten the word to the artist and "I hope the news will reach him in time to save you the annoyance to which you allude."

By that time the division of the properties had been agreed upon, and Goodnight had not done well. In part that was because he undercut any bargaining power he might have had by spending the entire time up to the final negotiations making clear his desperation to get out of the partnership, and denigrating the ranching economy. With reference to one potential buyer for Quitaque, in October 1886, Goodnight had remarked bitterly: "I don't think you can expect or look for honest men. Those kind will neither buy nor recommend purchase of a ranch in Texas now. We are looking for a party who can get up a first class swindle and carry it through." He also constantly warned of the impending deluge of settlers that would come with the completion of the railroad from Fort Worth to the Panhandle, expected in the fall of 1887. He had visions of "a regular stampede of emigrants [*sic*] to our ranches."

Mrs. Adair, a canny businesswoman with great experience in landholding in the United States and the United Kingdom, took the long view. She was not pressing him to sell out, but if he insisted, it would be on her terms. Goodnight made clear that he sought his one-third of the land in the western part of the Palo Duro, but the partnership contract gave her first choice if it were dissolved, and she apparently had the final say on how the boundaries of the divisions were drawn.

Although there is no record of the negotiations concluded May 21, 1887, we do know that she retained the entire Palo Duro Ranch of 336,000 acres and 48,000 head of cattle. She also continued to hold the Tule Ranch, which had never been part of the partnership, although Goodnight had managed it. He ended up with the Quitaque, consisting of 136,963 acres on the Llano, and valued at $2.25 per acre, plus 18,616 head of cattle and 140 horses and mules. Goodnight also assumed a mortgage on the Quitaque. He did not come out well in the negotiations with Maquay, who handled the settlement for Mrs. Adair. Regardless, he now owned land valued at about $260,000 and livestock worth at least another $180,000, plus he received an additional $24,000 for services previously rendered. Goodnight realized that he had been had, and two months later remarked bitterly in a letter to Maquay, "You have made your last sharp deal."

Although Mrs. Adair had chosen to divide the properties so that she might retain the entire Palo Duro Ranch, Goodnight made one last effort to buy the western end of the canyon. He described it as the "poorest land" and said he would "price it accordingly," but again she disappointed him. He did reluctantly consent to remain temporarily as manager of her properties, although he made clear the strain he was under. For him the worst part was being responsible for all the finances that required him to borrow money to meet ranch expenses, and respond to her demands for income from the property.

The drought continued unabated and several of the largest ranchers east of them were forced into bankruptcy. Thousands of acres, and Goodnight estimated 75,000 cattle, went under the hammer at sheriffs' sales. On one trip to Kansas City he approached every bank with which he had done business and "couldn't raise a dollar." He finally was able to sell four thousand yearling steers for $12.50 a head, and he got that price by soliciting a dummy bid from a friend that got the price up fifty cents, a stratagem that he was embarrassed to admit. That fall Maquay had directed Goodnight to send him $5,000, and $15,000 to Mrs. Adair. He could only respond that he would send it if he was able to sell enough cattle to raise that amount.

Throughout these tumultuous times, Goodnight was not a well man. In December 1886, he had complained of "getting too old and worn out." By October 1887 he reported to Maquay: "My digestion is entirely gone and I am having one hard spell a week. I expect to get away as soon as possible to be treated." And he did in November, apparently to Mineral Wells, back in Palo Pinto County, a spa famed for its mineral waters, guaranteed to cure any ailment.

He had another monthlong respite at the spa planned for early 1888. The visits to Mineral Wells seem to have helped Goodnight, at least he was confident that they had. If nothing else he learned that he must vary his diet, which throughout his adult life had featured strong coffee, beef, and beans. He also smoked cigars or chewed tobacco constantly. On the positive side, the decline of his responsibilities following the dissolution of the partnership could only have had a beneficial effect on Goodnight's health.

In late September 1887, Goodnight told Mrs. Adair that he wanted to give up the large ranch house that he and Mary had occupied for many years, and move to his Quitaque Ranch. At issue was whether or not the Palo Duro foreman should take over the home and assume the responsibility that the Goodnights had carried to provide hospitality for important visitors. For example, they had housed the official who classified state land as farm or grazing, with the latter being less expensive. The rancher made the case that befriending the man was in their interest as he had classified very little of the canyon acreage as agricultural. Goodnight, however, did not move out of the house until late December, when he finally severed all ties with Mrs. Adair and her properties.

Goodnight moved quickly to reduce his investment in the Quitaque, finding the rare person willing to invest in ranches at that time, L. R. Moore of Kansas City, with whom he closed a deal in October 1887. But even that operation resulted in some acrimony when Mrs. Adair was slow in delivering the deeds on the ranch, and Goodnight threatened to sue her.

The breakup of the Adair-Goodnight partnership ended the most productive decade of his life. With his relentless drive and expertise in all areas of ranching, coupled with the Adair financial resources, he had been able to put together a model ranching empire with title, or access, to 1.3 million acres in the Panhandle. Goodnight also had demonstrated his superior talents as a cattle breeder, producing some of the finest animals in the area. Sometimes, as the result of his being the manager and part owner of one of the largest cattle operations, he was drawn into activities for which he was less well suited. He undoubtedly made his presence as a lobbyist well known in Austin, but it is difficult to imagine him successfully playing the role of the facile, opportunistic representative of an industry. Certainly he never seems to have been at ease in that role. In later life he once commented that he did not engage in social drinking, nor did he gamble, and always felt like a fifth wheel with his peers. Now he was about to embark on a period in which he would be free to make his own decisions — but without the backing of Cornelia Adair's resources and financial acumen.

CHAPTER 10

Last Years as a Rancher

CHARLES Goodnight's activities between 1888 and 1919 are not well documented. Those who later interviewed him at length were primarily interested in his earlier careers as Ranger, cattle drover, and trail maker. We do know that while in the process of breaking away from the Adair connection he had begun to put together the Goodnight Ranch, which at its peak included over 40,000 acres, plus several thousand more leased, all north of the JA Ranch. When the Fort Worth and Denver Railway built through the area in 1888, it located a station near the center of his ranch and named it Goodnight. A small community developed there, on the outskirts of which was constructed an impressive two-story home that Goodnight designed and whose construction he supervised.

The rancher sent the carpenter he employed, at the substantial salary of one hundred dollars a month, to Louisiana to select the lumber for the house. Goodnight had the hardwood doors made in Trinidad, Colorado. According to two Texas Tech University professors of architecture, the house, which survives to this day, contains 2,900 square feet, plus a 361-square-foot basement. All of the rooms have nine-foot ceilings, and one of the bedrooms on the second floor has a large sleeping porch. This afforded Goodnight an opportunity to sleep under the stars, something to which he had become inured during his cattle driving days. With its ample porches, stained-glass bay windows, and five chimneys, the house is an imposing sight, even in its present dilapidated condition. Unoccupied now, it can be seen a hundred yards south of U.S. 287, about forty miles east of Amarillo, near a historical marker lauding

Charles Goodnight: "Trail Blazer, Indian fighter and who established the first ranch in the Texas Panhandle in 1876 and is known as the Burbank of the Range."

The house at Goodnight remained his home until 1927, but his stake in the ranch gradually shrank. About 1895 he sold interests in it to two businessmen, and the short-lived Goodnight-Thayer Cattle Company was born. In 1899 Thomas Bugbee, whom Goodnight had barely beat out for the title "First Rancher in the Panhandle," bought a half interest in the ranch, and in 1900 another businessman purchased all but ten thousand acres. Goodnight's years as a serious rancher had come to an end. But he had developed another and more risky interest, silver mining in Old Mexico.

Exact dates are not known, but around 1890 Goodnight and three partners acquired presumed rights to a mine in the southern part of the state of Chihuahua. He spent a rigorous five months at the mine site, working like a peon, he said, but in vain. In the last year of his life Goodnight remembered bitterly the experience: "My greatest financial blow, was the loss of our mine in Mexico. I had the best Mexican lawyers examine the title to it, and they pronounced it sound. Then some people came in and exercised a mortgage on it and secured it. That cost me a little over three hundred thousand dollars and forced me to sacrifice property that would have made me millions."

Despite his losses, throughout the period the Goodnights were generous to a fault, particularly in the area of education, which probably reflected Mary's many years as a teacher. They provided financial assistance to more than a dozen young people who left the Panhandle in search of an education, and in 1897 they founded Goodnight College in the village. "Academy" might have been a more accurate title as it initially limited enrollment to 125 and academically was essentially a high school. The Goodnights first built an administration building and a dormitory with the intention of ultimately turning it over to one of the denominations to administer, but Methodists and then Baptists failed to make a success of it. Then it became an orphanage, until the administration building burned. Goodnight retrieved the bell from the tower of the main building and later donated it to the Panhandle-Plains Historical Society, with the wry comment that it was all he had to show for a $75,000 investment.

The Goodnights' contributions to education in the Panhandle, however, were not forgotten by those whom they had helped. In 1929 one of them, whom Charles and Mary had aided by providing room and board in exchange for chores around ranch headquarters, recalled a tongue-lashing Goodnight had given him. His crime was dulling an axe while cutting kindling "on the ground instead of on a log. I have never," declared the man, "forgotten the scolding and it has been a good lesson to me through all these years." He was proud to inform Goodnight that he was drawing a good salary at a lumber yard, and had several rental properties.

Goodnight's venture into higher education attracted a lot of attention, as did the man himself in the nineties, because the people of Texas began to look back with nostalgia on the era of free range and long cattle drives, symbolized by no one more than Charles Goodnight. He was featured prominently in the *Historical and Biographical Record of the Cattle Industry and the Cattlemen of Texas and Adjacent Territory,* published in 1895. Indeed, it declared that "the name of Charles Goodnight is perhaps more extensively known than that of any other Western cattle owner of the present-day." Well over half of the article was devoted to his early exploits as scout for Ranger units, and to his post–Civil War career driving herds to New Mexico and as far north as Wyoming. His role as an industry innovator also was recognized: "Mr. Goodnight has devoted much of his time to a thorough study of cattle breeding and handling, and has introduced many new methods and practices." His pioneering work in cow spaying was singled out for particular commendation, as was his leadership in cattlemen's organizations. That he was currently president of the Bank of Clarendon warranted mentioning, and the only really false note was the statement that Goodnight "has always stood aloof from politics." That hardly comported with his prominent role in the great fight over the "children's grass." Finally, he was described as "free from all desire for notoriety." With the passage of time, however, he would come to enjoy the limelight, while vociferously denying it.

Ten years after the publication of the *Historical and Biographical Record*, a similar volume with an odd title appeared, *Poetry and Prose of the Livestock Industry*. Published by the National Livestock Historical Association of Kansas City, it encompassed the entire Great Plains and included material on sheep, goats and swine, as well as cattle. Only forty-four individuals were singled out for biographical treatment, but they included Theodore Roosevelt and Charles Goodnight. The latter was described as "one of the greatest all-around cattlemen who has ever lived upon the Plains." The writer, James W. Freeman, had personally interviewed him and obviously had been impressed. He not only had sat by Goodnight's fireplace as the old rancher reminisced, but Freeman had also ridden around the ranch with him while Goodnight expounded on raising cattle and the care and perpetuation of his buffalo herd, "an animal with which his name will always be inseparably connected."

His work with buffalo led to a correspondence for over twenty years with officers of the American Bison Society, headquartered in New York City. Initially he communicated with Martin S. Garretson, the secretary, with whom he had become acquainted in the 1880s, and who visited the ranch on more than one occasion. By the 1920s Goodnight also was corresponding frequently with Edmund Seymour, president of the society. Indeed, another officer once made a request of Seymour: "Please do not send Mr. Goodnight's letters. I have not time to read them. And I am afraid he will wear *you* out by much writing." The man whose remarkable energies had been tasked to administer ranches with 100,000 cattle spread over 1.3 million acres, while simultaneously heading a major lobbying effort in Austin, now had too much time on his hands.

His friend and fellow rancher, Tom Bugbee, managed to accumulate a small fortune and expended some of it in sightseeing. He saw much of the United States, and also visited South

America, Hawaii, the Philippines, Japan, and China. In contrast, Goodnight eventually did go to California or Arizona during the winter months, but otherwise he found that the Panhandle offered enough for a full life. His tolerance, however, did not extend beyond state lines. He had a poor opinion of Oklahomans, a feeling shared by those occupants of the Panhandle today who hold that making jokes at the expense of the rest of Texas is unnecessary as long as Oklahoma is handy.

Blessed with all that energy and an inquiring mind, Goodnight was incapable of vegetating. He was fascinated by nature in all of its manifestations. As a scout, he had learned how to find water by observing patterns of bird activity. His experiments with plants and animals earned him the nickname Burbank of the Range, but a trained scientist he was not, and his experiments and theorizing reflected this. For example, he maintained that as longhorns moved to higher altitudes their horns shrank in size, something no other student of the breed confirmed.

Over the years, Goodnight invested much time, energy, and resources trying to create a viable new breed, cattalo, by crossbreeding buffalo and Angus cattle. For the new animal he made many claims, among them, immunity to cattle diseases, and a requirement of less care and food, while producing more meat and living longer. At the height of his interest in the cattalo, he had a herd of over a hundred, representing different degrees of crossbreeding, but he ultimately became so discouraged at the frequency of abortion that he was encountering—virtually no bull calves survived—that in 1917 he began to sell them off. That coincided with a dispute as to the relative roles of Goodnight and one Buffalo Jones in the development of the cattalo.

Jones was a picturesque character who had achieved national celebrity by his vendetta against hunters. Intent on saving wildlife, he earned his own credentials as a sportsman by lassoing, and then releasing, everything from cougars and grizzly bears to African lions and zebras. His unusual approach to hunting earned him a bonanza of publicity, every minute of which he enjoyed. He spoke at dinners hosted by sportsmen, and attended by local reporters, and was always in costume, clad in buckskin, as he told of his exploits. And he was not above exaggerating to make a good story better. One example that Goodnight found particularly aggravating, as did Martin Garretson, had Jones capturing three buffalo calves and riding off with them. His critics thought one would have been a load, and three impossible to handle.

It was Edmund Seymour, of the bison society, who had precipitated the quarrel between Goodnight and Jones. He was interested in the history of the cattalo, and had conflicting accounts from the two men. To resolve these differences he shared each man's correspondence with the other. That included a letter in which Goodnight suggested that Jones, who had been an employee of the Park Service at Yellowstone, had swallowed too much hot air from a regional weather phenomena, the chinook, a warm, southerly breeze.

Seymour also informed Jones that Goodnight had ridiculed his claim that he had participated in a capture of Billy the Kid. The Panhandle Stock Association, with Goodnight in a leadership role, had hired John W. Poe to go to New Mexico to assist Sheriff Pat Garrett with the Billy the Kid problem. Goodnight advised Seymour to contact Poe, then living in New Mexico, to verify his charge.

There was an exchange of letters between the antagonists about the role of each in the development of the cattalo, and Buffalo Jones's claim to have participated in the arrest of Billy the Kid. Neither gave much ground, although Jones kept protesting that he had only the highest opinion of Goodnight. Some resolution was achieved, and two years later, Jones died. Goodnight had the good fortune to outlive most of his antagonists.

After Goodnight's own death, Martin Garretson commented at length on the controversy, contrasting the flamboyant Jones, with his talent for self-promotion, with Goodnight, who "disliked praise or publicity . . . was strong for correct statement and detail even at the expense of reducing his own connection with certain events to a minor part or eliminating himself altogether."

In 1918 Goodnight still owned 115 cattalo, 170 buffalo, and

Charles Goodnight, ca. 1910. He has come on to bad times, principally because of bad investments. Courtesy Panhandle-Plains Historical Museum, Canyon, Texas.

135 karakul sheep, although he was about to put his ranch on the market and give up his animal breeding experiments. One that had disturbed some people was his breeding a sow with a ram, something he had heard happened by chance in Mexico. He reported that cholera, a serious disease for swine, was no problem for the new breed, and that its meat would be less inclined than pork to cause indigestion. Goodnight acknowledged, "I think I am considered by all that know me a little 'locoed.'" He did get a few litters from the cross, but the man who ultimately took over the ranch killed the survivors, and Goodnight made no further attempts to pursue the project.

He also made no effort to tamper with the bloodlines of his fine flock of sheep. He did propose to blend their unique wool with buffalo hair to make a new cloth. And he sent some buffalo hair to Taos Indians with whom he was acquainted, and they wove him a blanket about one-third buffalo hair.

Goodnight had expected a blanket of 100 percent buffalo hair and concluded that the Indians had reserved some for their own use. However, he forgave them: "I shouldn't have blamed them if they had stolen it all, as they certainly have a prior right to buffalo." He never forgot that he and other white men like him had dispossessed these first Americans.

His active mind also led him to engage in medical experiments. "I have made it a point during my life trying to understand every thing that pertains to a cow," Goodnight once wrote. Nor did he neglect the bulls. On long drives, he had observed that they sometimes became crippled by pain from their scrotums banging against their legs. To remedy this, he developed an operation by which he moved the testicles higher up the scrotum, tying off and amputating the lower part, thus reducing the arc of its swing. When he reported his novel procedure he was ridiculed by some, but, "I have followed it on animals for many years and it served its purposes." It should be no surprise that his enthusiasm for medical innovations carried over to his fellowman.

In 1916 Goodnight revealed to Edmund Seymour that he had discovered remarkable qualities in salve made from buffalo tallow. He had cured one of his own corns and a lame knee with applications, and also brought relief to one of his tenants with a bad back. In addition it could be used, he declared, to clean silver and paintings and, "I am satisfied it will relieve rheumatism. I do believe it works. . . . Give it a test in behalf of humanity," he pled. Referring to its use by Indians, he concluded, "We would like to know as much as the Indian."

Ten years later Goodnight was still convinced of the medicinal benefits of buffalo tallow, and he finally found a convert in Dr. W. K. Fouts, of Dallas, who advertised his company as "Specialists of Chronic Diseases of Men, Women and Children." Martin Garretson of the bison society, to whom Goodnight had turned for help, reported that several laboratories had been unable to find medicinal value in the tallow. Dr. Fouts, however, who had "studed [*sic*] Bactorlegy [*sic*] for years," became convinced that it was all Goodnight claimed. In his own laboratory Fouts had found in tallow traces of phosphorus, iron, calcium, soda, magnesium, potash, silica, and sulfuric acid.

Dr. Fouts was not sharing his findings with the medical profession, but was "experminting" [*sic*] on the poor people. He discovered that it was effective on a wide range of illnesses, from pneumonia and tuberculosis to cancer. The good doctor was happy to report that one of his deaf patients had heard — for the first time in thirty years — the post office clock strike. And, "I am going to take a few boxes out to the orphans' home and let them try it on babies that had croup, bad colds, and coughs." Hopefully, the children survived the treatments.

During World War I, Goodnight did not offer buffalo tallow to the army medical corps, but he did send a pair of buffalo-hair socks to warm General John J. Pershing's feet during the European winter. And he had some ideas on how to properly arm our cavalry, but these were shared only with Seymour. Based on his experience in the Rangers and conversations with Civil War veterans, he advised arming cavalrymen with four Colt revolvers. He reminded Seymour that effective use of the lance and saber depended upon the strength of the individual, whereas "the six shooter man is equal. . . . Cavalry can easily carry four pistols," Goodnight declared, "and those twenty-four shots can easily carry anybody they charge." (Before we scoff at this advice, we should recall that as late as the bloody Battle of the Somme in 1916, the British High Command held cavalry units in reserve, ready to exploit the expected rupture of German lines by artillery and infantry.)

Shortly before the United States entered the war, Goodnight got involved in an effort to produce a movie. The idea for a film of Indians hunting buffalo originated with J. L. Lackey, an attorney at Claude, about ten miles west of the village of Goodnight. He had attended a buffalo hunt Goodnight staged on his ranch for Indians. The rancher had provided a single animal, yet as word spread of the impending event, a large crowd descended on the ranch to watch the hunt. Lackey was impressed by the interest the event engendered and conceived the idea of having a film crew present for a repeat performance. Goodnight initially rejected the idea, but after a few days to reflect, concluded, according to Lackey, that "it would be both profitable and of great historic value."

Before filming began, Goodnight, and the few Indians old enough to have hunted buffalo, planned the action, and the rancher then "instructed" the director and cameraman. The camera crew came from Denver, and the Kiowa Indians from the former Kiowa, Comanche, and Apache Reservation in Oklahoma. There were the inevitable expenses, including transporting and feeding the Indians. Goodnight had to provide the several hunters with bows and arrows, the fabrication of which had become one of his hobbies. As the Indians no longer wore breechclouts, someone decided to substitute drawers such as men were wearing as underwear at that time. To the best of his ability, Goodnight staged the hunt to replicate those he had seen in the old days, but the sight of those underwear-clad Indians charging up and down the hills made it more of a Mel Brooks production.

By the time the movie was ready for distribution, World War I entertainment taxes had killed any chance of it being shown in theaters, at least that is what one Chicagoan that Lackey contacted had concluded. Despite the film fiasco, Lackey was lavish in his praise of Goodnight, who had "the most active and quickest working mind of any man I ever met of his age, forms his ideas in an instant, and answers quick." Lackey also spoke of Goodnight's extensive charity work, describing him as "always for the right . . . is today almost in a class by himself." Goodnight sent a copy of the film to Seymour in New York in the hope that he could find an outlet for it in the city, but in vain. Goodnight found himself stuck with two thousand dollars for expenses incurred during the filming.

In his enthusiastic letter to Seymour, Lackey mentioned another thing that he found interesting in Goodnight, his "very strong [belief] in the subconscious mind, and the influence it has over people, who will admit to its action." Both Goodnight and Mary were afflicted with the variety of health problems that accompany the aging process. His hearing and sight were slowly deteriorating, and she was having mental health problems. In his eighties, he traveled to Glen Rose, Texas, to the Snyder Sanatorium, which featured masseurs who were reported to have cured several cases of blindness. After a few days there, in a fit of optimism, he reported, "It now appears fairly certain that they will cure me." Unfortunately that was not to be.

He also was attracted to parapsychology, or what he referred to as "free knowledge" and "distant treatment." The latter he confessed to having "much faith in." And he offered Martin Garretson advice on how to practice it. "If any of your acquaintances or friends have a nervous habit concentrate your mind on them for a while with the aid of your subforces [sic]. . . . I am quite sure I have cured people in that way." But the "subforces" were of little avail in money matters.

Goodnight's financial situation was slowly deteriorating. Saddled with $60,000 of debt, in 1918 he began to look for a buyer for his ranch. At one point he hoped to interest Martin Garretson and Edward Seymour. To them he spoke of the possibility of striking oil or gas on the land, and the certainty that the "cattle business is bound to be the best of all at the end of the war," a prediction no rational economist would have made. He was on sounder ground when referring to potential gas and oil discoveries. After all, within thirty-five miles of his property some ranchers had hit it big and were rapidly becoming wealthy. Goodnight did have at least one well drilled on his property, but the return was too poor to keep it pumping. As early as 1915 Goodnight had tried to lease oil rights on some of Cornelia Adair's acreage, but she had rebuffed him. To T. D. Hobart, then managing her properties, she justified her refusal: "Dear Mr. Goodnight is very sanguine and speculative and liable to be taken in. He has lost almost all of his fortune in that way. . . . At the same time I am very anxious to help him. . . . But I don't want to encourage him in any 'wild cat' schemes."

He continued to be optimistic about the possibility of a big strike on his land, but when he finally had an offer for his ranch he had to take it. The transaction involved his remaining 3,773 acres, the main house, and two tenant houses. The livestock included 170 head of buffalo, 115 cattalo, and 135 karakul sheep. Later, Goodnight declared that he had sold "for a low figure," $160,000, but there were other provisions in the contract. He would be permitted to retain ownership of a gray horse, named Dick. More important, Goodnight would be allowed to occupy his home as long as he wished. In addition, he was guaranteed a "portion of all meats butchered on the ranch, such garden truck and fruit grown thereon as he may reasonably need, and the use of such milk cows as deemed necessary." He also retained half of the mineral rights and would be paid a nominal sum for managing the ranch for the new owner. Finally, the contract allowed Goodnight to manage the celebrated buffalo herd that had begun with four calves that he and a brother-in-law had captured and that had attracted national attention. The actual care of the herd Goodnight delegated to his foster son, Cleo Hubbard, whose widowed mother had been his housekeeper.

Most men in their eighties would have been content to rest on their laurels and enjoy a quiet semiretirement, but not

Goodnight. There was a growing interest in the pioneer days of the cattlemen, in which he had played such a prominent role.

Indeed, there was also evidence that the man was becoming history conscious and interested in helping write the story of post-1860 West Texas, in which he had played such an important role.

CHAPTER 11

The Rest of the Story

BY the 1920s there was a growing interest in the historic role
that the early Panhandle settlers had played. Even as early as
1916 Charles Goodnight had suggested to T. D. Hobart, Cornelia Adair's ranch manager, that at the next reunion of Panhandle old settlers they consider launching an historical society.
The idea had originated just a few days earlier at a meeting at
Goodnight's attended by several people, including his old
friend, Oliver Nelson; a former antagonist, James N. Browning; and Laura Hamner, a local historian and journalist.

Goodnight's interest may have been sparked by his affiliation
with the recently founded Old Time Trail Drivers' Association,
affiliated with the Texas Cattle Raisers' Association, of which he
had been a member since 1886. John R. Blocker, the first president of the Trail Drivers', had taken his own first herd north in
1873 and his last twenty years later. He described the association's mission as keeping alive "the memory of the old trail
drivers. . . . To stimulate it, and keep alive in the hearts of our
Texan youth, will inspire a spirit of reverence and gratitude to
their historic fathers for the liberty which they have given them
—for the free institutions which are the result of their daring."
A bit fulsome, but Texans are not noted for understatement.

One of the first acts of the association was to invite submis-
sion of reminiscences, and they came in a flood. Goodnight's
contribution was "The Killing of Oliver Loving," included in
the association's two-volume publication, *The Trail Drivers of
Texas*.

Another local effort was to persuade Congress to fund the
purchase from Cornelia Adair of a portion of the Palo Duro

Canyon and set it apart as a national park, complete with the Goodnight buffalo herd. The leader in this venture was Mary Goodnight, who, backed by others, was able in 1916 to get the local congressman to introduce a bill for that purpose. However, it died in committee.

This rise in interest in monuments to their recent past was not surprising. Panhandlers were proud of their role in opening Texas's last frontier. Also, as a result of their disputes with the state government over public land use, the people of the Panhandle had developed a feeling that they were not only different, but superior. Some of that persists to this day, which has led writer Paul F. Starrs to pass on the observation: "If Texas is a state of mind, the Panhandle is a state of grace." Goodnight, for one, was convinced that the Panhandle environment produced better cattle, and if that were true, "Why shouldn't it produce better men?" Such attitudes helped launch a regional historical society.

Goodnight did not have a personal role in the founding of the Panhandle-Plains Historical Society, but was close to acquaintances who did. Moreover, personnel of the new society regarded him as a potentially valuable source of artifacts for their museum and for recollections important for the region's history. The lead articles of the first and third numbers of the *Panhandle-Plains Historical Review,* which began publication in 1928, were "Charles Goodnight's Indian Recollections," and "Charles Goodnight, Pioneer," both by J. Evetts Haley, the journal's editor. The driving force behind the founding of the historical society had been Joseph A. Hill, the first chairman of the History Department of the West Texas State Teachers College, at Canyon. His initial contact with Goodnight had come in 1916, when the president of the college suggested that he call upon Goodnight, who had checked in at a Canyon hotel. Hill's intent was to invite the rancher to contribute artifacts to a hoped-for museum at the college. Hill recorded that Goodnight's instant and forceful refusal "bowled me over with his abruptness and the picturesqueness of his easy-to-understand language," apparently a euphemism for a torrent of profanity.

In 1921 Hill and other faculty and students organized the Panhandle-Plains Historical Society. By this time Hill had become president of the college, and Lester F. Sheffy had succeeded him as chairman of the History Department. It fell to Sheffy, the first president of the society, to approach Goodnight for support. He found him sitting on the ground repairing a gate that did not meet the Goodnight standard. After it became apparent that the rancher was not going to recognize his presence, Sheffy took the initiative: "Colonel Goodnight, my name is Sheffy." The response was quick and to the point: "I don't give a damn what your name is. What the hell do you want?"

With the conventional courtesies out of the way, Goodnight invited the shocked professor to accompany him back to the house, where he showered Sheffy with ten pictures of pioneer Panhandle days, plus a set of Luther Burbank's collected works. These were the first items in what would become the valuable Goodnight Collection at the Panhandle-Plains Museum.

But Goodnight did not develop a close relationship with the society until the summer of 1925, when J. Evetts Haley, who had just graduated from West Texas State, accepted the position of field secretary for the society. The position required Haley to contact people who might have artifacts or personal reminiscences that could help tell the story of the Panhandle's early years. Haley's first contact with Goodnight came shortly after he had assumed his position. A decade later he recalled vividly that he had "hesitatingly crossed his ranch-house yard to face the flow of tobacco juice and profanity." The old rancher did not tolerate fools gladly, but he quickly recognized that in the young field secretary he had someone who knew and loved ranching and was committed to recording the life that Goodnight had lived.

That summer Haley had several interviews with Goodnight, covering a variety of subjects, mostly relating to cattle drives. Included, however, were accounts of Goodnight's entry into the Palo Duro, and his journey the next year from Trinidad to Palo Duro accompanied by Mary and the Adairs. He also spoke to the topic of cattle drives out of the Panhandle to Dodge City.

Goodnight's statement on this subject, dated June 5, 1925, merits quoting in its entirety, as it demonstrates the amount of information and opinion that he could distill into one paragraph.

FIRST HERD OUT OF THE PANHANDLE

The first herd we drove from the Panhandle was driven by Leigh Dyer to Dodge in 1877. It was a beef herd. Even though our beeves were good Colorado cattle they were cheap and I don't think brought more than 2 1/2 or 3 cents a pound. We used twelve or fourteen men on the trail. We used about four guards at night but sometimes only three and again only two. We used the Dipper as a guide to tell how long to stand guard as we had no watch. The last guard was usually the shortest for each man would stand a little overtime to be sure he watched long enough. There were no skunks on the cow outfit. The cowboys were the highest class people and they saved Texas. It usually took about twenty-two days for the drive to Dodge. We would make about a twelve mile drive each day.

Haley enrolled at the University of Texas, where in one academic year he earned a history M.A., writing a thesis under the tutelage of Eugene C. Barker, the university's Texas history authority. The topic was the cattle drives from Texas to northern markets after the Civil War, a natural for a student who had learned to love the cowboy life on small ranches his businessman father owned.

While in Austin, Haley continued to draw upon Goodnight for information, asking him to respond by mail to questions. Haley's many questions to Goodnight seem to have convinced him that he did have a responsibility to share his knowledge of the old days. Moreover, he must have enjoyed the opportunity to relive those days on the trail. At least two articles, "Managing a Trail Herd in Early Days," and "First Entrance to Palo Duro Canyon," appeared under his name in the Amarillo *Southwest Plainsman and Panhandle Weekly*, in November and December 1925. Nearly ten years later, Cleo Hubbard, his foster son, testified that Goodnight had dictated to him the account of the entry into the Palo Duro, and he probably was responsible for getting his foster father in print on both occasions. At the time, Hubbard was managing the buffalo herd that the new owner of the ranch had agreed to permit Goodnight to continue to hold. Laura Hamner, who knew the family well, portrayed a close relationship between the Colonel and his foster son.

There was a growing interest in the buffalo herd and its owner. Among those attracted was J. Frank Dobie, who had recently rejoined the English Department at the University of Texas. Twelve years older than Haley, he had had even greater ranching experience than the field secretary. Dobie had actually been born and reared on a ranch, and had left the University of Texas in 1920 to manage a ranch in southwest Texas owned by an uncle, Jim Dobie. Returning to the university after a year, Dobie found an intellectual home in the Texas Folklore Society, and a career as a commentator on Texas history and culture.

In August 1926 Dobie wrote Goodnight, reminding him that they had met earlier that year in San Antonio at a reunion of the Trail Drivers' Association, and asking permission to interview him about "the trailing of cattle out of Texas." Dobie had already obtained from *Country Gentleman* a statement of interest in an article on Goodnight. To convince Goodnight of his bona fides, the professor stated: "I am the son and grandson of trail drivers, and uncles on both sides of my house have been cattlemen." Goodnight replied promptly with a brief message agreeing to be interviewed, although adding, "I have no desire to appear in print." This was despite his having already been the author of the two articles in the Amarillo newspaper, and the subject of glowing chapters in the two volumes previously cited.

Dobie did interview Goodnight over a period of several days. Apparently the two got off to a bad start, at least from the Colonel's perspective, and after the first day he was speculating about how to terminate the interview. The relationship, however, took a turn for the better, and the two men became quite friendly. Dobie later described the experience in a chapter of his

Cow People. "He was plainly not elated at my arrival, though courteous enough," reported Dobie. "He told me right off that he did not care a damn for any 'publicity' that I or any other writer could give him." At supper, Dobie was impressed by the "biggest bottle of pepper sauce I have ever seen — red Mexican peppers in maybe two quarts of vinegar." Goodnight ate rapidly, without saying a word, and then left the table, explaining, "I was never a hand to dally about the table, excuse me."

Over the next few days, the professor was completely captivated: "I developed a positive admiration for him as a man of large nature, wisdom, concern for other people, and a noble sense of values." And his article in *Country Gentleman* opened with, "Beyond all doubt the most remarkable trail blazer and frontiersman now living in the Southwest, if not in America, is Charles Goodnight." In another article composed for *Country Gentleman,* but which its editor rejected, Dobie addressed the topic, "Charles Goodnight Observant Man," and described him as "the best educated man that I have ever met," defining an educated man as "one who can view with interest and intelligence the phenomena of life about him. . . . To talk with him on anything he has looked at," declared Dobie, "the buffalo, the longhorn, the prairie dog, the antelope, the mesquite, the Pecos River, the dove, the prairie chicken — is to hear poured out a wealth of intimate detail that the most acute scientist might overlook."

Dobie also found it possible to extenuate Goodnight's irascibility: "The gruffness is partly habit. It is partly an expression of sincere contempt for pretension, for hypocritical cant. More than anything else it is a mask to conceal one of the most sensitive, generous natures in the world." This is a remarkable tribute coming from a man who had a rather jaundiced view of his fellow man.

Dobie noted that the meals he had with Goodnight were prepared by a housekeeper, as Mary had died the previous April. She had been in ill health for several years and at one point her husband had resorted to the Weltmer Institute, which apparently practiced parapsychology, to treat her.

Back in 1922 Goodnight had decided to "commemorate Mrs. Goodnight and Mrs. [Thomas] Bugbee and the fortitude and courage they had to stay with their husbands in a country so remote and wild as the Panhandle of Texas was when they first entered it." The vehicle was to be clocks suitably inscribed, and he asked Martin Garretson to contract for them in New York. Somewhere along the way Mrs. Bugbee's was dropped, but Mary's clock finally arrived, complete with Goodnight's inscription:

IN HONOR OF MRS. MARY DYER GOODNIGHT
PIONEER OF THE TEXAS PANHANDLE

For many months, in 1876–1877, she saw few men and no women, her nearest neighbor being seventy-five miles distant, and the nearest settlement, two hundred miles. She met isolation and hardships with a cheerful heart, and danger with undaunted courage. With unfailing optimism, she took life's varied gifts, and made her home a house of joy.

In the summer of 1921, Martin Garretson had helped Goodnight take Mary, "who was afflicted with a severe nervous ailment," to a clinic in Nevada, Missouri. Nearly a decade later Garretson remembered Goodnight's deep solicitude for her and his remarking, "What would I do without her?" J. Evetts Haley provides a poignant description of the bereft husband, unable to bring himself to observe the complete funeral service, and returning to his lonely home. Given his own deteriorating health, it seemed probable that it would not be long before he joined her in the cemetery outside the village of Goodnight.

On November 1, 1926, Haley wrote Dobie, with whom he had become acquainted during his academic year in Austin. They were corresponding about their mutual interest in establishing the exact routes of trails Goodnight had pioneered. He informed "Mr. Dobie," that, "I hear that Colonel is very sick, and I am afraid will not pull through, but certainly hope so." Nine days later, Dobie responded with the news that he had recently received a letter from Goodnight, and "he says he is recovering."

Indeed he was recovering, and Haley spent a day and a half with him in mid-November. He reported that the Colonel had even been able to walk a little, and "seemed able to smoke as many cigars and drink as strong coffee as ever." Haley also observed that Goodnight's mental faculties had not suffered: "He is a real thinker, and his mind, in spite of his illness, is still as smart as a whip."

Haley also alluded to the possibility of literary competition in the form of Laura Hamner, the old acquaintance of the Goodnights. The daughter of a newspaper publisher in nearby Claude in the early nineties, she already was the author of many journalistic pieces about local people and events. She had been interviewing Goodnight before Haley came on the scene, and he feared that she already had some material that he was seeking, declaring, "Miss Hamner has the best log of his trails that has ever been laid off." But Haley, as a newly minted M.A. in history, took comfort in surmising that Hamner's "treatment will be of the romantic sort; and while I believe the historical would be much better, still there may be room for both."

In the same letter, Haley mentioned "a young lady cousin of the Colonel who has been with him about three weeks." This was Corrine Goodnight, a young woman who had contacted Goodnight several years earlier, after learning that she shared a surname with a celebrated frontiersman. A railroad telegrapher in Montana, by 1926 Corrine's curiosity had been sufficiently piqued by their desultory correspondence that she decided to stop by, en route to a vacation in Florida, and meet her possibly distant cousin. She arrived October 23 to find Goodnight seriously ill and the prognosis for recovery not good. He insisted that she extend her visit, and he did recuperate rapidly.

Corrine became not only his nurse, but as he resumed his heavy correspondence, his secretary, typing letters and responding to queries from Haley and Dobie. In a lengthy postscript to a Goodnight letter to Dobie early in February 1927, she identified herself as a nine-year employee of the Northern Pacific whose fourteen years in Montana had been "very sad ones." Within her first four years there, her father, mother, and a sister died, she and a younger brother being the sole survivors. She had cared for her sibling for eight years, helping him through public school and business college, and she was proud that he currently was a cashier in a Montana bank. She informed Dobie that she was twenty-six, and "I have tasted some of the Stern Realities of life and still can SMILE and feel that Life is mighty worth while and wonderful."

An attractive young woman with dark brown, wavy hair, Corrine once said that she had not been without beaux in Montana. Certainly having a bright, cheerful, and attractive young woman as his nurse and secretary reanimated Charles Goodnight. That she should have become enamored with a man about to celebrate his ninety-first birthday is more difficult to comprehend. Nevertheless, her correspondence and a diary that she began January 1, 1927, is replete with affirmations of her love and respect for the man old enough to be her grandfather.

As for Goodnight, the "Little Girl," as he referred to her, seems to have given him a new lease on life. She also must have been behind his sudden decision, early in February 1927, to move from the ranch house, which had been his home for nearly forty years, to a small bungalow in Clarendon. Corrine's first entry in her diary included, "I've had such a profound feeling of contentment since the day I arrived in October." Following the move to Clarendon, another entry listed things that she had failed to include in the move: "Left his tobacco there on purpose!" Already she was undertaking to remove some of the rough edges from this elderly male project.

His friends over his many years must have been astounded at the transformation they were witnessing. Corrine noted in Goodnight a new passion for cleanliness, and he asked her to comb his hair "several times a day." She also was enlarging his social circle. Early in February, for example, they drove to Amarillo, where they hosted a dinner at the Kansas City Waffle House. Their guests were Oliver Nelson, Laura Hamner, and two others. It is difficult to believe that Little Girl had already converted the Colonel, as she always referred to him, into a model of dining decorum, but at least she must have kept him at the table. Certainly he and Oliver Nelson never seemed at a loss for topics of conversation.

Laura Hamner later recalled an Amarillo parade in which the Armstrong County float featured a model of the first JA ranch house, with Goodnight seated at the entrance. Before the parade got underway he spotted Nelson in the crowd and persuaded his friend to join him. "Spitting and talking," they ignored the parade bystanders and rode the entire route deeply engaged in conversation. Two other things of which we can be certain were that Goodnight was not wearing cowboy boots or a gun belt for the parade. Goodnight always wore heavy work shoes, and he never carried a sidearm after he quit the long cattle drives. That explains Hamner's choice of *The No-Gun Man of Texas* as the title for her biography of him.

Corrine's diary reveals other, gentler sides of the man. She read to him constantly, as his eyesight had deteriorated to the point that he could no longer read. And she seemed genuinely gratified with "the contentment and happiness we find here." Throughout February there was diary evidence of an intensification of their relationship, despite his bouts of asthma. On the eleventh she recorded that he was feeling better, and "says to me repeatedly, 'Never in my life have I wanted to live as much as now and I want to make money for you.'" That inspired her to add, "Bless his dear heart, he has felt this way about life and me since the first he ever saw me — even though he was on the brink of Eternity."

Three days later she confided to her diary that he did not want her to leave, and offered himself to her. She added, "I've never had any doubts or fears in regard to our happiness. . . . We have talked it over for some time . . . but we find it a bit hard to set a date, etc." That, however, was soon resolved. The morning of March 5, the Colonel's birthday, he called his nephew, Henry Taylor, the mayor of Clarendon, to ask him to come to the house. On the mayor's arrival, Goodnight, somewhat belligerently, announced that he was going to get married that day. But he relaxed when the nephew quietly responded, "Fine.

How about marrying at my house?" Two hours later a minister performed the ceremony. The next day Corrine resigned from her position with the Northern Pacific, and recorded in her diary the end of her telegrapher days: "Good-night Dots and dashes."

The news of the marriage quickly spread across country. A ninety-one-year-old man acquiring a twenty-six-year-old bride was news. Even the *New York Times* devoted a few lines to the marriage: "Colonel Charles Goodnight, pioneer landowner and known as the Father of the Texas Panhandle." Closer home, the *Kansas City Star* sent a reporter to interview the newlyweds. Most of the article was devoted to summarizing the career of the "Noted Trail Blazer" and "Father of the Texas Panhandle," but the reporter did not ignore the "attractive" Mrs. Goodnight. She was quoted as saying, "The Colonel is a wonderful man," and "I find nothing strange in the difference in our ages. I have led a strange life anyway."

A Texas newspaper illustrated its long article on the couple with pictures of them, the Goodnight ranch house, and the Colonel on horseback. The reporter coined another nickname, acclaiming Goodnight "the Cecil J. Rhodes of the Southwest." As usual, however, the bulk of the story was a summary of his career as Ranger, cattle drover, and rancher, with references to the death of Loving, Luther Burbank, and Goodnight College. It concluded: "So at 91 this contemporary of Kit Carson, 'Joe' McCoy, Col. C. C. Slaughter, 'Shanghai Pierce,' 'Ike Pryor,' John Simpson Chisholm and other noted characters of a pioneer day is resting quietly, a bridegroom who is threatened to be spoiled by his alert companion."

The day following the marriage, Corrine wrote nearly identical letters to Dobie and Haley, announcing the event. She referred to "the Greatest Romance Texas Land has ever known," and stated, "All here . . . seem heartily glad to welcome and claim as their own the Montana Girl as the bride of the worthy and distinguished Colonel Charles." She concluded, "I shall continue to do everything in my power to bring all the love, sunshine and happiness possible into his precious life." Haley commented to Dobie, "Colonel Goodnight stole a march on us. . . . I suppose the Colonel is young enough to take another wife." Apparently he was, as Corrine very soon was pregnant.

The Goodnights' marriage inspired hundreds of congratulatory messages from all over the United States. Despite the deluge, Corrine continued to find time to keep her diary. On January 19, she noted that the Colonel "tells me some very wonderful and interesting things about his scientific discoveries," what he called Goodnighting. They included the "merits of Buffalo tallow" and his innovative operation on bull scrotums. April 27 she stated: "In evening enjoy exchanges of thought on various subjects. Religion — Womanhood, Manhood. Sex power — Passion. His scientific use of this led him to be well preserved at 80." She returned to that topic May 31, commenting on a discussion by Goodnight, which included the observation, "Passion and sex the foundation of accomplishment if rightly used and controlled and applied. Creative purposes only." Her entry for April 30 included the revealing, "[Goodnight] has felt modest and timid in meeting big people because of being mortified by lack of education." The brusque demeanor he exhibited in dealing with strangers may have been, in part, a reaction to his own feelings of inferiority.

Certainly the marriage had reinvigorated him. To a query from Edmund Seymour, he responded: "As to air castles, and what I am going to do: I have enough laid out ahead to keep me busy for the next twenty-five years at least, and I hope to live long enough to carry out every one of them."

Goodnight was now even more conscious of his financial limitations, and was casting about for ways to remedy them. Back in the early days he and his partner John Wesley Sheek had lost substantial numbers of stock to Indians he identified as Comanches. In 1891 Congress had authorized victims of Indian depredations to sue tribes in the Court of Claims. Sheek and Goodnight filed suits that resulted in Goodnight being awarded some $13,000, substantially less than he had sought. Nevertheless, even that minor victory in the courts must have encouraged him thirty years later to become involved in efforts to obtain a pension for his Ranger service, and to realize on an old Mexican land claim.

Goodnight solicited aid from Dobie to buttress his claim that he had done Ranger service. This venture may have originated with a Washington attorney who had concluded that Congress might be persuaded to award pensions to those, like Goodnight, who had been Rangers just prior to the Civil War. That was not a likely scenario, but the Colonel asked Dobie to try to locate muster rolls and "every particle of evidence you can scratch up for me." Nothing came of it, and the associated expenditures further depleted his financial resources.

He continued to confirm Cornelia Adair's evaluation of him as "very sanguine and speculative." Sometime in the mid-twenties, Goodnight and two others formed the Interstate Land Company with Goodnight as chairman, to try to realize on an old Mexican land grant. It was one of several associated with the name of John Charles Beales, an Englishman whose marriage to the widow of a Mexican land speculator with a large estate launched him on a long and complex series of land transactions. Beales was a frequent litigator in both Mexican and American courts, and only someone with Goodnight's desperate optimism would have tried to revive claims in Colorado that had eluded men wealthier and with more legal savvy than he. Nevertheless, with new family responsibilities, he began to call on Dobie and others to assist the Interstate Land Company to unearth documents in Texas archives that would strengthen its case. In the absence of more information, one might conclude that, as had been the case with the Ranger pension, only the lawyers would profit.

Goodnight's principal advisor in the Interstate Land Company affair was a Mr. Malone, described in Corrine's diary as "a very remarkable character. Striking and compelling personality." One bit of evidence of his financial acumen was his use of Goodnight's telephone, rather than his own, to place calls to England in a fruitless attempt to get information on settlers on a Beales grant. Malone also was given Goodnight's personal papers, apparently to be the basis of a never-written biography.

Charles Goodnight and Cornelia Adair, ca. 1920. He is facing financial problems that she attributes to his lack of business savvy. Courtesy Panhandle-Plains Historical Museum, Canyon, Texas.

J. Evetts Haley spent much time and effort trying to recover these papers before the mysterious Mr. Malone, but the papers disappeared from the scene. While the Colonel was having his financial problems, neither he nor Corrine was in good health. He had bad asthma attacks and by the end of March, her pregnancy was not going well. Her diary reported her bedfast some days, but her husband continued to be "kindness and goodness, 'Personified.'" When able, Corrine continued to handle the Colonel's correspondence and took dictation on the "history" that he was relating for Haley. They also found time to discuss prenatal care, and on that topic, "he has such splendid ideas about these things. Should have a mighty fine Kiddie. Sure do want him bad enough."

At the end of May they moved to another address in Clarendon. She enjoyed their new home, but her bouts of illness increased, and her diary entries ceased June 21 and did not resume until August 9. Sometime during that period she must have suffered the miscarriage that Goodnight would report to Dobie. Her last diary entry was August 28, and it was followed by a brief comment: "Have been in bed all summer and not able to keep up the Diary. I regret it exceedingly."

Meanwhile, Haley had been unable to devote much time to interviewing Goodnight. Most of his energy was going into an authorized history of the XIT Ranch, for which he was being paid by the month. He asked Frank Dobie to critique the finished manuscript, and he consented. Among Dobie's many observations in his devastating commentary was, "You will never make a historian until you learn to write." Actually, Haley had a colloquial style most historians would envy.

With the XIT manuscript completed, Haley returned to his Goodnight project. For some time, he had been puzzling over its format. Early on he had conceived it in terms of a history of the westward movement of the Texas frontier, for which the Colonel would be a prime source, as well as a leading participant. In early January 1929, however, Haley approached the Colonel with a proposal to do "a history of the Northwest

Charles Goodnight and J. Evetts Haley, 1927. Haley is fresh out of college and eager to make the acquaintance of the Panhandle's icon, who is showing his age. Courtesy Panhandle-Plains Historical Museum, Canyon, Texas.

Texas frontier, the cattle trails of the west, and something of Panhandle development, grouping all of this around your life." As rationale for this approach, Haley cited his pleasure with their association, the significance of Goodnight's accomplishments, the interest of other old-timers in a biography of the Colonel, and how it would advance the objectives of the Panhandle-Plains Historical Society.

Goodnight's response was prompt and positive. He rationalized that, although he had agreed for Malone to write his biography, Haley was proposing to write a "history of the Northwest Texas frontier in which I am interested." He even argued that "the settlement of the Panhandle, is unequal to anything in the United States," because it was "settled under more difficulty and expense." Moreover, "not only the vast number of criminals in this territory was against us but politically the whole state . . . placed burdens and difficulties which was not placed upon any other frontier." Like pioneers on other frontiers, the Colonel believed his was unique. He cited its "speed in settlement," and that "its great investments in churches and schools and other branches of civilization per capita surpasses anything ever known or heard of in America," an appraisal difficult to document.

Haley now had a green light to proceed, but continued to be worried about Malone and Laura Hamner. She, however, ceased to be a threat when she wrote Haley that she would have to undergo an operation and suspend indefinitely her project. Haley commented to Goodnight that this "is certainly unfortunate for her," but evidenced some relief that "it leaves a clear field for work along the lines you have agreed upon." Malone made his own contribution by simply disappearing, but taking the Goodnight papers with him. In June 1929 the Colonel and Corrine concluded a contract with Haley by which they pledged to provide him "the history of his life and something of the history of the Panhandle," and he agreed to give them a one-third interest in all royalties from the sale of the book.

That summer Goodnight continued to support the collection program of the Panhandle-Plains Museum, mounting buffalo horns for a rack to display bows and arrows that he had previously made and donated, and contributing a lariat. In the same period he found himself in the awkward position of having promised the museum a saddle that he already had lent to Cleo Hubbard, who was using it to work the Goodnight buffalo herd. Haley did assure the Colonel that "we do not want you, however, to go to any more expense in collecting these articles, as I am afraid you are doing more than you can afford."

Meanwhile, Haley was busy editing the second volume of the *Panhandle-Plains Historical Review,* and negotiating a new position in Austin. He would become an employee of the History Department of the University of Texas, with the assignment to collect historic materials, in much the same fashion as he had as field secretary for the Panhandle-Plains Historical Society. The position would be funded by a grant to the university, and Haley would be based in Austin while traveling throughout West Texas. He apparently had done little writing on his Goodnight project, and the travel required by his new position certainly would not be conducive to that effort. But it did give him the opportunity to further explore the region he loved, and contact its inhabitants, including the Indians of Taos Pueblo.

Goodnight and Haley shared an interest in the Taos Indians. The Colonel had employed a few as trail hands and subsequently gave the pueblo the foundation for a small buffalo herd. Haley, an avid hunter, had accompanied Taos Indians in forays into the high country of the Sangre de Cristo Range. Goodnight did not hunt, but was a great admirer of the Taos Indians and defended their right to practice their own religion. "I regret to have to say it is a purer article than we have," he once wrote, "and don't bother anyone but the Catholics." Nor did he have the typical Texan's hostility to the Comanches and Kiowas, whose raids had created so much havoc on that state's frontier, and had cost Goodnight himself thousands of head of cattle. Nevertheless, he helped them in a variety of ways, and until the creation of the Wichita Mountains Game Preserve's buffalo herd in 1911, Goodnight's buffalo were a magnet that drew Indians to see once again the animals that had made their old way of life possible. He maintained good relations with a number of Comanches and Kiowas, and Quanah Parker, the celebrated Comanche chief, only a month before his death, sought help from his old friend, "Mr. Charlie." He was planning to bring about fifty Comanches to "see your buffalo and make these old Indians glad."

Goodnight's sympathy for the Indians is further illustrated by a story he told Harley True Burton, the author of *History of the JA Ranch*. Goodnight had ridden into Clarendon one day in the early eighties to find excited local citizens surrounding and preparing to assault several Indians who the white men believed to be wild Comanches. Goodnight quickly recognized them to be Taos Pueblos, who were greatly relieved at the intercession of their old friend. Seeking an explanation for their being in Clarendon, Goodnight learned that they had descended the Canadian River to trade with the Kiowas, but had decided to return by a more direct route, and had become lost. To the rancher's query as to how they had become lost, given their centuries of experience with the Llano Estacado, the leader of the Indians responded frantically: "Alambre! Alambre! Alambre! todas partes!—Wire! Wire! Wire! everywhere." Of the white men present, apparently only Goodnight could comprehend their quandary and empathize with these Indians whose ancient trails had been blocked by the white man's wire fences.

During the 1928 Christmas season, Goodnight sent buffalo meat to Indian friends in Taos, and earlier that year he had taken them two buffalo robes. In addition, he was providing at least moral support to the Pueblos' unsuccessful campaign for a federal government land grant to provide a permanent home for the small buffalo herd he had given them.

In his last years the Colonel found that moving to a drier climate in the winter spared him severe asthma attacks. In 1928 he and Little Girl established residence in Phoenix, from which he sent a letter to the Clarendon newspaper lauding the "perpetual sunshine which is very warm but in no way oppressive." He also was struck by the depth of the fertile soil, which, coupled with irrigation, "is perfectly adapted to the growth of citrus fruit." Ever sanguine, Goodnight described Phoenix as "the throbbing heart of the most successful irrigation project in the world." (It can be assumed that Corrine contributed more to this letter than taking dictation.)

The following winter the Colonel and Corrine shifted to Tucson, and he soon was declaiming to Haley on the virtues of his new residence. "It is an ideal place on the edge of the city," he wrote. "We have a good view of the desert and mountains. . . . I am feeling fine and think we will like it better here than at Phoenix." Corrine added a postscript about the novelty of traveling with a celebrity: "No matter where we stopped on entire trip we met someone who knew Colonel."

Corrine was still at work reshaping this tough old codger to her vision of a proper husband. Although Mary had been a devout Christian, the Colonel did not become a member of a church until he remarried. During their second winter in Arizona, Corrine persuaded him to join an evangelical congregation of "the Apostolic faith." When Goodnight announced his conversion to his friends, he liked to point out that Mary also had espoused this denomination. People of this faith were not expected to be baptized, but the Colonel had been reared in a culture that identified church membership with baptism and insisted on it: "I am going the whole hog, I mean to go under the water." As his old friend Laura Hamner described it, the baptism took place in a cattle tank on one of the ranches in the vicinity: "The minister came to his side, spoke the solemn words, and buried under the water the brave old man, ninety-three, who met baptism as he met all things, alone, unafraid."

Death came to him in Tucson, December 12, 1929, presumably the result of the heart and lung problems that had plagued him for years. Corrine brought him home by railroad to be interred in the cemetery on the outskirts of Goodnight. It was a beautiful day; according to newspaper reporters, "a bright sun warmed the earth and occasionally soft puffy clouds drifted lazily under a turquoise sky." A line of automobiles two miles long made up the funeral cortege. Overhead was an occasional plane to remind the mourners that Goodnight's life spanned many decades. He had lived long enough to have Little Girl read him the newspaper articles describing Lindbergh's flight to Paris.

Two ministers preached at his funeral, as Haley described it in a letter to Frank Dobie: "Thank God you weren't here, and they were ten times as bad as I could have imagined. . . . They couldn't add, had they been the best, to the feeling of the crowd that gathered." Nor was he alone in these sentiments. "That ain't the kind of funeral for an old cowman like Charlie," complained an elderly cowboy. And another concurred: "I'll say not. The idea of preaching over Charlie!"

Hopefully, they were happier with the tall tombstone later erected, which carried a brief tribute to the Colonel and Mary: "Together they conquered a new land and performed a duty to man and God. He was a trail blazer and an Indian scout. She was a quiet home-loving woman. Together they built a home in Palo Duro Canyon in 1876. They developed the cattle industry. They fathered higher education and civic enterprises. To them the Panhandle pays reverent and grateful tribute."

Epilogue

EVEN as he lay at peace beside Mary, Goodnight's stature as a Panhandle icon continued to grow. A few months after his death, J. Frank Dobie lauded him as having been "the most romantic man living, not only in West Texas, but in the entire West. He was the most observant man I have ever known, and his life had compassed about all the experiences that the prairies, and thickets, and mountains of the West offered." Nor did Goodnight's hold on Dobie slacken with time. Several years later he declared: "I have met a lot of good men, several fine gentlemen, hordes of cunning climbers, plenty of loud-braying asses and plenty of dumb oxen, but I haven't lived long enough or traveled far enough to meet more than two or three men I'd call great. That is a word I will not bandy around. To me Charles Goodnight was great-natured."

But the Texas scholar who did the most to establish Goodnight's reputation was J. Evetts Haley, whose biography of him was published in 1936. Reviewers were uniformly laudatory. In the *Southwestern Review,* Dobie described it as a "great book . . . a resurrection literal in its fidelity and a creation based on penetrating interpretations." Savoie Lottinville, editor of the University of Oklahoma Press, which printed or reprinted virtually all of Haley's books, judged *Charles Goodnight* to have been "the best Plains biography ever written."

Haley estimated that to get his original publisher, Houghton Mifflin, to accept his manuscript he had had to cut it one-third, most of that from Goodnight's "later days." Like Dobie, Haley found most interesting Goodnight's roles as Ranger, trail blazer, and cattle drover.

When Haley had been trying to decide whether to attempt a biography of Goodnight, and get his cooperation on the project, he had been concerned about Laura Hamner, who already had been interviewing Goodnight, and was a family friend of long standing. The serious illness, mentioned earlier in this text, had forced her to interrupt her research. Nevertheless, she did later resume the project and in 1935, a year before Houghton Mifflin issued Haley's work, she published privately in Amarillo *The No-Gun Man of Texas,* aimed at the public school market. The following year she produced a trade edition, and both Haley's work and hers were reviewed in the same issue of the *Panhandle-Plains Historical Review.* Haley's rated the lead review by Lester Sheffy, the editor. He stated that "few men are better versed in the language of the cowmen and the plainsmen than is Haley. He speaks their language." He concluded that Haley had produced a biography that "will live long among the biographies of men."

In contrast, *The No-Gun Man of Texas* was assigned to a Mrs. Everett Carpenter of Amarillo, who devoted part of her review to Hamner's treatment of Mary Goodnight and contented herself otherwise with summarizing the book. She did not mention that Hamner, in an effort to give her work authenticity, had included in an appendix two comments from Goodnight. In one dated January 28, 1928, he had written: "I am returning your manuscript. I believe you now have all correct information and you will be in a better position to write a better book about our early years of the cattle business than any one else. . . . Don't hesitate to call on me for any information, for it gives me great pleasure to be of assistance to a very dear friend." In the second one, dated January 22, 1929, Goodnight declared, "am so delighted with the first draft of your book."

Hamner gave more attention than did Haley to Goodnight's last thirty years, but only relatively so. That period, while significant, is slightly depressing. The aging cycle had taken its customary physical toll, although he remained as alert mentally as a man many years his junior.

That longevity contributed to his stature is clear. He simply outlived his cohorts. Of the eighteen men who had made the drive from Palo Pinto County to Fort Sumner in 1867, he was the sole survivor after the death of Bose Ikard, in early 1929. Of the prominent ranchers who had entered the Panhandle before 1880, none outlived him. Thomas Bugbee, who also retired to Clarendon, was a greater financial success than Goodnight, and was about six years younger, but he died four years earlier. Henry W. Cresswell had been associated with Goodnight in ranchers' organizations in both Colorado and the Panhandle, and has been described by H. Allan Anderson as a "range cattleman with few equals and no superiors." He died in 1904 at the age of seventy-eight. Leigh Dyer, one of Mary's brothers, was thirteen years younger than Goodnight, and worked with him, off and on, for twenty years, and died in his fifties. And David T. Beals, only about four years older than Goodnight, entered the Panhandle a year later and quickly developed the highly successful LX Ranch, which he had the good fortune to sell for about $1.5 million in 1884. That was just before the financial crisis that rapidly eroded Panhandle cattle and land prices. Beals wisely invested the proceeds from the sale of the LX, and when he died, in 1910, he was a wealthy man. Goodnight, however, could have found satisfaction in his outliving Beals by two decades.

Longevity, however, was only a part of what made Charles Goodnight a Panhandle icon. As the founder of one of the largest ranches in the area, and always active in promoting ranchers' interests, he was the best-known Panhandle rancher in Austin, loved by many back home, and hated by some. Part of his visibility can be attributed to his physical presence, a solid two hundred pounds and six feet tall, at a time when most men were several inches shorter. This impressive physique was supplemented by an agile mind, amplified by a sharp tongue. Those meeting him for the first time, like those two West Texas State College faculty members, Joseph Hill and Lester Sheffy, were usually stunned by the volume and speed of his delivery — and his profanity. Goodnight was an intimidating presence.

But there were other sides to the man. He inspired confidence, and other men who shared his views of what was best for the big ranchers were happy to accept his leadership. By the 1890s, however, the tide had turned, and voters with a few cattle and small acreages in wheat or cotton had begun to outnumber the large ranchers and their employees. And the new power bloc had the support of the local newspaper editors, who knew that their financial interests lay with the burgeoning farm population.

It is fair to speculate about the importance of the John George Adair connection on Goodnight's career. Undoubtedly, Adair's ability to produce the capital to buy strategic parcels of land enabled the partners to control adjoining acreage, fence it, drill the wells, and construct the tanks. Adair funds also bought the high-grade Hereford bulls to upgrade the herds. Without these financial resources, Goodnight may well have been in the ranks of those ranchers whose creditors in the mid-eighties forced them into sheriffs' sales. After all, it had happened to Goodnight in Colorado. Even with the support of Adair, he found the management burden unbearable. But he was able to liquidate his one-third interest and emerge a moderately wealthy man by Panhandle standards. Unfortunately, he rather quickly dissipated most of his capital and was forced to end his ranching career by 1920.

During the 1920s, Goodnight voiced a number of times his regret at being unable to be as charitable as he once had been. He and Mary had enjoyed sharing with others, and the extent of their generosity undoubtedly has contributed to the burnishing of his image as a Panhandle icon. Nor should the great publicity attendant on his marriage to the twenty-six-year-old Corrine be ignored. The *New York Times* was not alone in referring to him as "the father of the Panhandle" in its coverage of the wedding.

Looking back in his old age, Goodnight concluded: "Taken all in all, my life on the trail was the happiest part of it." Given his personality, that must have been the case. In those years he was totally in command. He determined when to get the herd moving, the pace, the direction it would take, and where and when to bed down at the end of the day. River crossings were undertaken when and where he felt best, and he usually led the way across. Crew members were carefully chosen and were compelled to abide by his rules. He was a hard and demanding boss, but the hands had confidence in his judgment. After a few drives he had a core of able men willing to follow his lead. Newcomers could either adapt to the Goodnight regimen, or leave.

As a rancher, he maintained the same high standards. Those capable and willing to meet his demands remained in his employ for years. But Goodnight no longer was totally in charge. He was the junior partner in a relationship that mandated that he seek approval for major financial decisions and produce a steady profit, or explain why not. It did not help that the people to whom he had to answer were in Italy or the British Isles, and communication could be delayed for weeks, despite cable connections. Goodnight was the same knowledgeable and effective ranch manager, but the constant pressure and acrimony were too much for him, and he left the partnership—on Cornelia Adair's terms. He was completely shut out of his beloved Palo Duro Canyon, the best ranching location in the Panhandle and his home for a decade.

After that, it had been downhill all the way. Nevertheless, Goodnight's standing in the public eye continued to grow. By the time of his death, in late 1929, he was being lauded as the Father of the Panhandle. If any man merited that title, it was Charles Goodnight.

Further Reading

Anyone interested in learning more about Charles Goodnight should begin with the biographies of him by J. Evetts Haley, *Charles Goodnight: Cowman and Plainsman* (Norman: University of Oklahoma Press, 1949) and Laura V. Hamner, *The No-Gun Man of Texas* (Amarillo, Tex.: 1936). I have depended most heavily on Hamner, a longtime friend of Goodnight who interviewed him extensively. He also read her first draft and expressed his satisfaction with it. Goodnight's second wife, Corrine, assured Hamner of the "pleasure he got out of reading your manuscript and in revising your notes." One of Goodnight's closest friends, Oliver Nelson, also read the manuscript and complimented Hamner on her work.

Additional sources on Goodnight are sketches in *Historical and Biographical Record of the Cattle Industry and the Cattlemen of Texas and Adjacent Territory* (St. Louis: Woodward & Tiernan Printing Co., 1895).

Goodnight's own "Recollections" are to be found in two repositories. The Panhandle-Plains Historical Museum in Canyon, Texas, has the first eighty-five pages, and the Haley Museum and Library in Midland, Texas, has the remaining 140. Both repositories have an abundance of other material relating to Goodnight.

At the University of Texas at Austin, the Harry Ransom Humanities Research Center holds the J. Frank Dobie Papers, and the Center for American History on the same campus has some Goodnight materials, including Corrine Goodnight's diary.

For the topography and early history of the Panhandle there are several valuable studies, including: Frederick W. Rathgen, *The Texas Panhandle Frontier* (Lubbock: Texas Tech University Press, 1998), John Miller Morris, *El Llano Estacado* (Austin: Texas State Historical Association, 1997), and Dan Flores, *Caprock Canyonlands* (Austin: University of Texas Press, 1990).

The Horsehead Crossing of the Pecos is best described in Patrick Dearen, *Crossing the Rio Pecos* (Fort Worth, Tex.: TCU Press, 1996).

Charles Kenner, "The Origins of the 'Goodnight' Trail Reconsidered," *Southwestern Historical Quarterly* 77 (January 1974): 390–94, discusses that controversial issue.

W. J. "One-Arm Bill" Wilson's account of his and Oliver Loving's fight with the Comanches appears in J. Marvin Hunter, editor, *Trail Drivers of Texas*. 2 vols. (San Antonio: Jackson Printing Co., ca. 1920–23): 348–53.

Further information on John Chisum (Chisholm) can be found in Harwood P. Hinton, Jr., "John Simpson Chisum, 1877–84," *New Mexico Historical Review* 31 (July 1956): 177–205.

The letter of the young Englishman from Palo Duro Canyon can be seen in Lowell H. Harrison, editor, "Wintering in Palo Duro Canyon, 1876–1877," *Panhandle-Plains Historical Review* 38 (1965): 46–51.

Byron Price provides a sound analysis in "Community of Individualists: The Panhandle Stock Association, 1879–1889," in John R. Wunder, editor, *At Home on the Range: Essays on the History of Western Social and Domestic Life* (Westport, Conn.: Greenwood Press, 1985).

For exaggerated claims for the Plains beef industry, see General James S. Brisbin, *The Beef Bonanza: Or How to Get Rich on the Plains* (Philadelphia: J. B. Lippincott & Co., 1881).

The time that Goodnight and companion found lodging for the night near Fort Elliott is depicted in Millie Jones Porter, *Memory Cups of Panhandle Pioneers* (Clarendon, Tex.: Clarendon Press, 1945).

A discussion of George Adair as an Irish landlord can be found in W. E. Vaughn, *Sin, Sheep and Scotsmen* (Belfort, UK: Appletree Press, 1983).

The subject of foreign capital investment in American ranching is covered in Gene M. Gressley, *Bankers and Cattlemen* (New York: Alfred A. Knopf, 1966), and W. S. Kerr, *Scottish Capital on the American Credit Frontier* (Austin: Texas State Historical Association, 1976).

A good description of the JA in 1880 is to be found in S. Nugent Townshend, *Our Indian Summer in the Far West* (London: Charles Whittingham, 1880).

Indispensable is Harley True Burton, *A History of the JA Ranch* (Austin: Press of Von Boeckman-Jones Co., 1928).

L. F. Sheffy, *The Life and Times of Timothy Dwight Hobart* (Canyon, Tex.: Panhandle-Plains Historical Society, 1950), has important things to say about the relations between Cornelia Adair and Goodnight in the early twentieth century.

Joseph A. Hill, *The Panhandle-Plains Historical Society and Its Museums* (Canyon: West Texas State College Press, 1955), provides insights on Goodnight's relations with that institution.

María E. Montoya, *Translating Property: The Maxwell Land Grant and the Conflict Over Land in the American West, 1840–1900* (Berkeley: University of California Press, 2002), discusses the Beales land grants, one of which Goodnight became involved in, in the 1920s.

Last, but not least, the six-volume *New Handbook of Texas* (Austin: Texas State Historical Association, 1996) has a wealth of information on numerous topics touching on a study of Goodnight and Texas ranching.

Index